11 DE MAYO DE 1992

CARLOS
FRANCO
ZESATI

Japanese
Grammar

by

Nobuo A~~~

Professorial Lecturer, Japanese Language
The Paul H. Nitze
School of Advanced International Studies
The Johns Hopkins University

and

Carol Akiyama

Language Training Consultant
Washington, D.C.

BARRON'S EDUCATIONAL SERIES, INC.

All inquiries should be addressed to:
Barron's Educational Series, Inc.
250 Wireless Boulevard
Hauppauge, New York 11788

Library of Congress Catalog Card No. 91-171
International Standard Book No. 0-8120-4643-9

Library of Congress Cataloging-in-Publication Data
Akiyama, Nobuo.
Japanese grammar / by Nobuo Akiyama and Carol Akiyama
    p. cm.
Includes index.
ISBN 0-8120-4643-9

    1. Japanese language—Grammar. I. Akiyama, Carol. II.
Title

PL533.A35 1991   91-171 CIP

PRINTED IN THE UNITED STATES OF AMERICA
1234 5500 987654321

Contents

Special Topics

Preface

This book is one of a new series of handy grammar reference guides designed for students, businesspeople, and others who want to improve their knowledge of Japanese grammar. It enables you to reflect on what you already know, to reinforce your skills, and to fill in the gaps.

Whether you are just beginning your study of Japanese or have some basic Japanese and want to refresh your memory, this book is for you. Previous knowledge has not been taken for granted; definitions and explanations are simple and concise, and examples use and reuse a core of basic vocabulary.

The book is divided into three section: The Basics, Parts of Speech, and Special Topics.

- In the Basics section you will find a nontechnical and easy-to-follow discussion of Japanese sounds, spelling conventions, and word-order patterns.

- In the Parts of Speech section you will find the nouns, particles, verbs, etc. that make up the Japanese language.

- In the Special Topics section you will find numbers, expressions for telling time, common conversation techniques, useful expressions, etc.

We would like to thank Masako Nanto, Foreign Service Institute, Department of State, and Diane Roth, editor, Barron's Educational Series, Inc., for their invaluable help with this project.

Nobuo Akiyama
Carol Akiyama

How To Use This Book

In the chapters that follow, a numerical decimal system has been used with the symbol § in front of it. This was done so that you may find quickly and easily the reference to a particular point in basic Japanese grammar when you use the index. For example, if you look up the entry "particles" in the index, you will find the reference given as §6. Sometimes additional § reference numbers are given when the entry you consulted is mentioned in other areas in the chapter §.

The Basics

§1.

Pronunciation Guide

§1.1 WHAT ARE VOWELS AND CONSONANTS?

There are two kinds of sounds in any language.

- *Vowels* are produced by air passing out through the mouth without being blocked. The letters that represent these sounds are **a, e, i, o, u**.

- *Consonants*, on the other hand, are produced by blockage (partial or complete) of the air. The remaining alphabet letters are used to represent consonant sounds: **b, c, d**, etc.

    Japanese isn't difficult to pronounce if you follow a few simple guidelines. Take the time to read this section, and try out each sound presented.

§1.2 VOWELS

If you have studied Spanish, it may help you to know that Japanese vowels are more like those of Spanish than English.

The following vowels are short and pure, with *no glide*— that is, they are not diphthongs.

JAPANESE VOWEL	ENGLISH EQUIVALENT	EXAMPLE
a	as in father	akai (*ah-kah-ee*) red
e	as in men	ebi (*eh-bee*) shrimp
i	as in see	imi (*ee-mee*) meaning
o	as in boat	otoko (*oh-toh-koh*) male
u	as in food	uma (*oo-mah*) horse

The following vowels are like the ones above, but lengthened.

JAPANESE VOWEL	ENGLISH EQUIVALENT	EXAMPLE
ā	as in father, but lengthened	batā (*bah-tah*) butter
ei	as in men, but lengthened	eigo (*eh-goh*) English
ii	as in see, but lengthened	iiharu (*ee-hah-roo*) insist
ō	as in boat, but lengthened	ōsama (*oh-sah-mah*) king
ū	as in food, but lengthened	yūbin (*yoo-been*) mail

Macrons

A *macron*, or bar, above a vowel means it should be lengthened.

EXAMPLE

butter / batā / *bah-tah*

In the above word, the macron above the second vowel means you should hold the sound twice as long as you normally would.

And keep in mind these points:

- Long vowels are important. Pronouncing a long vowel incorrectly can result in a different word or even an unintelligible one.

  For example, obasan (*oh-bah-sahn*) means **aunt**
  obasan (*oh-bah-sahn*) means **grandmother**

  ojisan (*oh-jee-sahn*) means **uncle**
  ojiisan (*oh-jee-sahn*) means **grandfather**

  seki (*seh-kee*) means **seat**
  seiki (*seh-kee*) means **century**

- Sometimes the **i** and the **u** aren't pronounced. This usually occurs between voiceless consonants (**p**, **t**, **k**, **ch**, **f**, **h**, **s**, **sh**), or at the end of a word following a voiceless consonant.

EXAMPLES

  sukiyaki   (*skee-yah-kee*)

This word for a popular Japanese dish begins with **skee**, not **soo**. The **u** is not pronounced.

  tabemashita (*tah-beh-mahsh-tah*) **I ate**

The **i** is not pronounced.

§1.3 CONSONANTS

With a few exceptions, Japanese consonants are similar to those of English. Note those that are different:

f   The English **f** is pronounced with a passage of air between the upper teeth and the lower lip. To make the Japanese **f**, blow air lightly between your lips as if you were just beginning a whistle.

g   Always as in **g**o, never as in a**g**e. You may also hear it pronounced as the **ng** sound in si**ng** but not at the beginning of a word.

r   This is different from the English **r**. To make the Japanese **r**, lightly touch the tip of your tongue to the bony ridge behind the upper teeth, almost in the English **d** position. It's more like the Spanish **r**, but it's not trilled.

s   Always hissed, as in **s**o, never voiced, as in hi**s** or or plea**s**ure.

And note the following points as well:

- If you have trouble making a consonant the Japanese way, your English pronunciation will still be intelligible.

- Some Japanese consonants are doubled. In English, this is just a feature of spelling and often doesn't affect pronunciation. In Japanese, the doubling is important and may change the meaning of a word.

EXAMPLE

Kite kudasai (*kee-teh koo-dah-sah-ee*) means **"Please put it (clothing) on."**

Kitte kudasai (*keet-teh koo-dah-sah-ee*) means **"Please cut it."**

In a word with a doubled consonant, don't say the consonant twice—simply hold the sound longer.

The Japanese Writing System

§2.1 DIRECTION AND CHARACTERS

Traditionally, Japanese is written from top to bottom and from right to left. But it is also written horizontally and from left to right, as in English.

Japanese writing uses three kinds of characters:

kanji (*kahn-jee*)	漢字
hiragana (*hee-rah-gah-nah*)	ひらがな
katakana (*kah-tah-kah-nah*)	カタカナ

Hiragana and katakana are also called **kana** (*kah-nah*). All three are used together in Japanese writing.

§2.2 KANJI

Chinese and Japanese are completely different languages. But beginning in the fourth or fifth century, Japanese adopted written symbols and many vocabulary items from Chinese. In Japan, these symbols or Chinese characters are called **kanji**. They represent both meaning and sound, and

6

often one kanji has more than one pronunciation (or reading, as it's commonly called) and meaning.

Japanese people learn about 2,000 kanji by the end of junior high school. Those are the basic characters used in newspapers, magazines, and school textbooks. Most Japanese know several thousand additional kanji as well.

Kanji range from simple, with one or two strokes, to complex, with many strokes needed to make one character. Some look like pictures, or line drawings, of the words they represent.

EXAMPLES

mountain	yama (*yah-mah*)	山
river	kawa (*kah-wah*)	川

These two together form Yamakawa, 山川 a family name.

Here are some more kanji:

Japan	Nihon (*nee-hon*)	日本 日本
person	hito (*hee-toh*)	人 人
	jin (*jeen*)	
Japanese	Nihonjin (*nee-hon-jeen*)	日本人

日本人

§2.3 HIRAGANA and KATAKANA

Hiragana and **katakana** symbols represent the sounds of syllables. Hiragana is used for native Japanese words and grammatical elements, and katakana is mainly for words of foreign origin. Each is a kind of alphabet, or syllabary, of 46 characters or sounds.

The following example will show you how the elements are used together.

Sumisu san, Nihon e yōkoso. / **Welcome to Japan, Mr. Smith.**
スミスさん、日本へようこそ。

Smith	**Mr.**	**Japan**	**to welcome**
Sumisu	san	Nihon	e yōkoso
スミス	さん	日本	へようこそ
katakana	hiragana	kanji	hiragana

The **hiragana** and **katakana** charts provided here will be useful if you continue your study of Japanese.

HIRAGANA

あ a (ah)	い i (ee)	う u (oo)	え e (eh)	お o (oh)
か ka (kah)	き ki (kee)	く ku (koo)	け ke (keh)	こ ko (koh)
さ sa (sah)	し shi (shee)	す su (soo)	せ se (seh)	そ so (soh)
た ta (tah)	ち chi (chee)	つ tsu (tsoo)	て te (teh)	と to (toh)
な na (nah)	に ni (nee)	ぬ nu (noo)	ね ne (neh)	の no (noh)
は ha (hah)	ひ hi (hee)	ふ fu (foo)	へ he (heh)	ほ ho (hoh)
ま ma (mah)	み mi (mee)	む mu (moo)	め me (meh)	も mo (moh)
や ya (yah)		ゆ yu (yoo)		よ yo (yoh)
ら ra (rah)	り ri (ree)	る ru (roo)	れ re (reh)	ろ ro (roh)
わ wa (wah)				を o (oh)

ん n				

が ga (gah)	ぎ gi (gee)	ぐ gu (goo)	げ ge (geh)	ご go (goh)
ざ za (zah)	じ ji (jee)	ず zu (zoo)	ぜ ze (zeh)	ぞ zo (zoh)
だ da (dah)	ぢ ji (jee)	づ zu (zoo)	で de (deh)	ど do (doh)
ば ba (bah)	び bi (bee)	ぶ bu (boo)	べ be (beh)	ぼ bo (boh)

ぱ pa (pah)	ぴ pi (pee)	ぷ pu (poo)	ぺ pe (peh)	ぽ po (poh)

きゃ kya (kyah)	きゅ kyu (kyoo)	きょ kyo (kyoh)
しゃ sha (shah)	しゅ shu (shoo)	しょ sho (shoh)
ちゃ cha (chah)	ちゅ chu (choo)	ちょ cho (choh)
にゃ nya (nyah)	にゅ nyu (nyoo)	にょ nyo (nyoh)
ひゃ hya (hyah)	ひゅ hyu (hyoo)	ひょ hyo (hyoh)
みゃ mya (myah)	みゅ myu (myoo)	みょ myo (myoh)
りゃ rya (ryah)	りゅ ryu (ryoo)	りょ ryo (ryoh)

ぎゃ gya (gyah)	ぎゅ gyu (gyoo)	ぎょ gyo (gyoh)
じゃ ja (jah)	じゅ ju (joo)	じょ jo (joh)
びゃ bya (byah)	びゅ byu (byoo)	びょ byo (byoh)
ぴゃ pya (pyah)	ぴゅ pyu (pyoo)	ぴょ pyo (pyoh)

KATAKANA

ア a (ah)	イ i (ee)	ウ u (oo)	エ e (eh)	オ o (oh)
カ ka (kah)	キ ki (kee)	ク ku (koo)	ケ ke (keh)	コ ko (koh)
サ sa (sah)	シ shi (shee)	ス su (soo)	セ se (seh)	ソ so (soh)
タ ta (tah)	チ chi (chee)	ツ tsu (tsoo)	テ te (teh)	ト to (toh)
ナ na (nah)	ニ ni (nee)	ヌ nu (noo)	ネ ne (neh)	ノ no (noh)
ハ ha (hah)	ヒ hi (hee)	フ fu (foo)	ヘ he (heh)	ホ ho (hoh)
マ ma (mah)	ミ mi (mee)	ム mu (moo)	メ me (meh)	モ mo (moh)
ヤ ya (yah)		ユ yu (yoo)		ヨ yo (yoh)
ラ ra (rah)	リ ri (ree)	ル ru (roo)	レ re (reh)	ロ ro (roh)
ワ wa (wah)				ヲ o (oh)
ン n				
ガ ga (gah)	ギ gi (gee)	グ gu (goo)	ゲ ge (geh)	ゴ go (goh)
ザ za (zah)	ジ ji (jee)	ズ zu (zoo)	ゼ ze (zeh)	ゾ zo (zoh)
ダ da (dah)	ヂ ji (jee)	ヅ zu (zoo)	デ de (deh)	ド do (doh)
バ ba (bah)	ビ bi (bee)	ブ bu (boo)	ベ be (beh)	ボ bo (boh)
パ pa (pah)	ピ pi (pee)	プ pu (poo)	ペ pe (peh)	ポ po (poh)
ファ fa (fah)	フィ fi (fee)	フ fu (foo)	フェ fe (feh)	フォ fo (foh)
キャ kya (kyah)		キュ kyu (kyoo)		キョ kyo (kyoh)
シャ sha (shah)		シュ shu (shoo)		ショ sho (shoh)
チャ cha (chah)		チュ chu (choo)		チョ cho (choh)
ニャ nya (nyah)		ニュ nyu (nyoo)		ニョ nyo (nyoh)
ヒャ hya (hyah)		ヒュ hyu (hyoo)		ヒョ hyo (hyoh)
ミャ mya (myah)		ミュ myu (myoo)		ミョ myo (myoh)
リャ rya (ryah)		リュ ryu (ryoo)		リョ ryo (ryoh)
ギャ gya (gyah)		ギュ gyu (gyoo)		ギョ gyo (gyoh)
ジャ ja (jah)		ジュ ju (joo)		ジョ jo (joh)
ビャ bya (byah)		ビュ byu (byoo)		ビョ byo (byoh)
ピャ pya (pyah)		ピュ pyu (pyoo)		ピョ pyo (pyoh)

§2.4 ROMAJI

The commonly used expression for the romanization of
Japanese words is **rōmaji**. Although there are several
systems of rōmaji, the most widely used, and the one used
in this book, is a modified version of the Hepburn system.

§3.

Word Order

§3.1 WHAT IS A SENTENCE?

A *sentence* is an organized series of words which
enables us to make a statement, ask a question, express
a thought, offer an opinion, and so forth. In writing, an
English sentence starts with a capital letter and ends with
a period, a question mark, or an exclamation mark. In
writing (using rōmaji), a Japanese sentence starts with a
capital letter, and ends with a period, not a question mark
or an exclamation mark.

EXAMPLES

Yoko is Japanese. / Yōko san wa, Nihonjin desu.
(statement)

Is Yoko Japanese? / Yōko san wa, Nihonjin desu ka.
(question)

Yoko, be careful! / Yōko san, ki o tsukete kudasai.
(exclamation)

§3.2 THE ENGLISH SENTENCE

English is a *Subject-Verb-Object* language. (So are French,
German, Spanish, and Italian.) This means that in a typical
sentence (a statement, not a question), the subject comes
first, the verb next, and the object last. This kind of word
order sequence for the sentence is sometimes referred to
by the initials **SVO** (an SVO language).

EXAMPLES

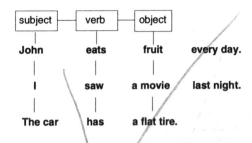

subject	verb	object	
John	**eats**	**fruit**	**every day.**
I	**saw**	**a movie**	**last night.**
The car	**has**	**a flat tire.**	

Understanding this principle of word order is important because, as we shall see in **§3.3**, the word order in Japanese is different.

English sentences have two basic parts, a *subject* and a *predicate*.

The subject is "who" or "what" the sentence is about. A subject must contain a noun or pronoun. In a statement, the subject is usually the first element in the sentence.

EXAMPLES

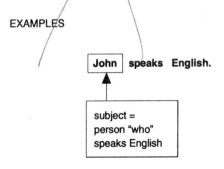

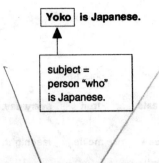

Yoko is Japanese.

subject =
person "who"
is Japanese.

- The predicate is that part of the sentence that expresses what is said about the subject. It usually can be found directly after the subject, it must include a verb, and it includes everything remaining in the sentence that is not part of the subject.

EXAMPLES

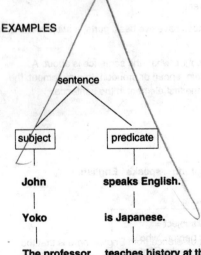

sentence	
subject	predicate
John	speaks English.
Yoko	is Japanese.
The professor	teaches history at the university.

§3.3 THE JAPANESE SENTENCE

§3.3-1 Subject-Object-Verb Sentences

Japanese is a *Subject-Object-Verb* language. (So are Korean, Mongolian, and Turkish). Thus, in a typical sentence, the subject comes first, the object next, and the verb last. This kind of word order sequence for the sentence is sometimes referred to by the initials **SOV** (an SOV language).

EXAMPLES

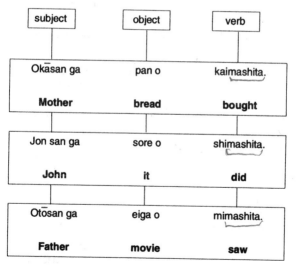

subject	object	verb
Okāsan ga	pan o	kaimashita.
Mother	**bread**	**bought**
Jon san ga	sore o	shimashita.
John	**it**	**did**
Otōsan ga	eiga o	mimashita.
Father	**movie**	**saw**

The significant difference from English here is that the verb must come at the *end* of the sentence.

- What about questions? The word order remains the same.
  But remember: Japanese does not use question marks. A
  sentence becomes a question by adding the particle *ka* at
  the end. You can think of *ka* as a question mark. (Particles,
  an important Part of Speech in Japanese, will be discussed
  in §6.)

  EXAMPLES

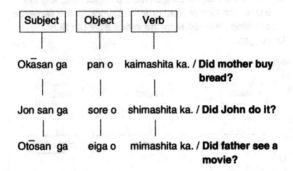

Subject	Object	Verb
Okāsan ga	pan o	kaimashita ka. / **Did mother buy bread?**
Jon san ga	sore o	shimashita ka. / **Did John do it?**
Otōsan ga	eiga o	mimashita ka. / **Did father see a movie?**

§3.3-2 Subject and Predicate

Japanese sentences *may* have a subject or a topic, but they
must have a predicate. (The subject is followed by the
particle *ga*, and the topic by the particle *wa*. See §6.)

- The *predicate* is the core of the Japanese sentence. It
  comes at the end, and it must be a verb or a verbal form. In
  Japanese, a verbal form may be a noun plus copula (like
  English **is** or **are**. See §7.6), or a verbal adjective.

EXAMPLES

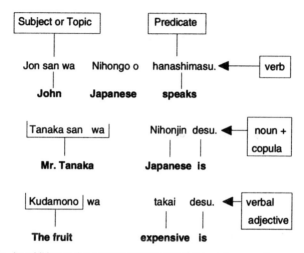

- In addition to the *subject* or topic, there may, of course, be other elements in the sentence—*object*, *indirect object*, *adverb*, and so forth. They come before the predicate, and are not considered part of it.

- Two principles hold true for word order in a Japanese sentence:

  The predicate must come at the end of the sentence.

  A particle must immediately follow the word or words it marks.

- Other than this, word order is not rigid. The subject or topic usually comes first, although an adverb of time may precede it or follow it. Expressions of time usually precede expressions of place. Most modifiers precede the words they modify.

EXAMPLES

Kare wa mainichi uchi de shinbun

he topic **every day** **home** at **newspapers**
    marker

o takusan yomimasu.

obj. **many** **reads**
marker

Kono kodomotachi wa Nihonjin desu.

these **children** topic **Japanese** **are**
          marker

Shinbun ga tēburu no ue ni arimasu.

newspaper subj. **table** **'s** **top** on **(there) is**
       marker

Kyō Jon san wa Tōkyō kara Kyōto ni ikimasu.

Today **John** topic **from** **to** **will go**
         marker

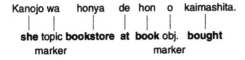

Kanojo wa   honya   de   hon   o   kaimashita.

she topic **bookstore** at **book** obj. **bought**
    marker   marker

- With a question, the word order is the same. As you now know, the particle *ka* at the end of the sentence makes a statement into a question.

EXAMPLE

Kanojo wa honya de hon o kaimashita ka. / **Did she buy a**
                                             book at the

she topic   **bookstore?**

- If a question uses a question word (*when, who, what*, etc.), it normally comes after the subject or topic, but this is not rigid.

EXAMPLES

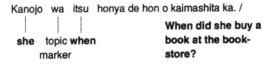

Kanojo   wa   itsu   honya de hon o kaimashita ka. /

                                     When did she buy a

she topic **when**   **book at the book-**
    marker   **store?**

Kanojo   wa   naze honya de hon o kaimashita ka. /

                                  Why did she buy a

she topic **why**   **book at the book-**
    marker   **store?**

Dare ga honya de hon o kaimashita ka. / **Who bought
a book at the
bookstore?**

who subj.
  marker

Sore wa donna hon desu ka. / **What kind of book is it?**

it topic **what kind of**
  marker

§3.3-3 Incomplete Sentences

In most languages, words that can be understood or implied
from the context of the situation can be left out of a
sentence. In Japanese, it is the subject or topic that is
omitted, not the predicate. If the situation is clear without the
subject or topic, Japanese tend to leave it out.

EXAMPLE

Kore wa nan desu ka. / **What is this?**

Kore wa hon desu. / **This is a book.**

or

Hon desu.

book is

In English, this question could be answered with just the
noun: **A book**.

In Japanese, the copula, or verb **to be** is needed too.
Remember, a Japanese sentence must have a predicate, or
verb form. Look at some more examples.

EXAMPLE

Anata wa nani o kaimashita ka. / **What did you buy?**

| | |
you what did buy

Although this sentence is gramatically correct, the Japanese prefer to omit the **you** which would be obvious from the context.

EXAMPLE

Nani o kaimashita ka. / **What did (you) buy?**

Hon o kaimashita. / **(I) bought a book.**

In a sense, these shouldn't be called "incomplete sentences" because, to the Japanese, they are quite complete!

Parts of Speech

§4.

Nouns

§4.1 WHAT ARE NOUNS?

A *noun* is a word that names or refers to a person, place, or a thing. A thing may be a quality or a concept.

There are two main types of nouns:

* A *proper* noun names a particular person, place, or thing. In English, all proper nouns are capitalized. The Japanese concept of proper nouns is more limited. In Romaji (see §2.4), names of persons or places, for example, are capitalized, but days of the week and months of the year are not. The word for other languages are capitalized, but not the word for English: *eigo*.

EXAMPLES

Jon san wa, Tōkyō ni ikimasu. / **John is going to Tokyo.**

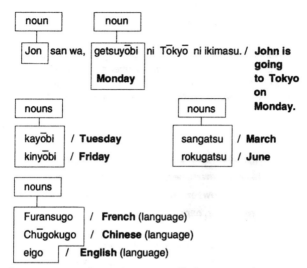

A *common* noun does not name a particular person, place or thing.

EXAMPLES

hon / **book**   otokonoko / **boy**   onnanoko / **girl**

§4.2 GENDER

Japanese nouns do not have *gender*. There are no special endings to show masculine, feminine, or neuter forms.

§4.3 ARTICLES

Japanese does not use *articles* before nouns. There are no words to correspond to English **a**, **an**, or **the**.

§4.4 NUMBER

Number means that a word can be *singular* (referring to
one person, thing, etc.) or *plural* (referring to more than
one). With most Japanese nouns, number is not an issue.
The same word is used for one or for more than one.

EXAMPLES

hon / **book, books**

shinbun / **newspaper,**

newspapers

kuruma / **car, cars**

uchi / **house, houses**

ki / **tree, trees**

te / **hand, hands**

Hon o motte imasu. / **I have a book.**

Hon o motte imasu. / **I have some books.**

- For nouns referring to people, the plural suffix *-tachi* may be
used, although it isn't required.

EXAMPLES

kodomo / **child, children**

otokonoko / **boy, boys**

onnanoko / **girl, girls**

hahaoya / **mother, mothers**

sensei / **teacher, teachers**

kodomotachi / **children**

otokonokotachi / **boys**

onnanokotachi / **girls**

hahaoyatachi / **mothers**

senseitachi / **teachers**

- When *-tachi* is used with someone's name, it usually refers
to the person and his or her family or group.

EXAMPLES

Tanaka san tachi / **Mr. Tanaka and his family**

Tomoko san tachi / **Tomoko and her group**

§4.5 NAMES

Japanese use *family names first*, and *first names last*.

EXAMPLES

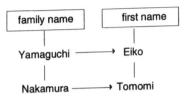

When Japanese introduce themselves to each other, they say the family name first. However, they know that English speakers do it the opposite way.

Japanese prefer family names, not first names. Japanese adults rarely use first names. Even among friends, family names are the rule, first names the exception. Unless a Japanese specifically asks you to use his or her first name, you should use the family name.

With children, it's different. Japanese use young children's first names followed by the title *chan*, older children's first names followed by *san* (see **§4.6**).

§4.6 TITLES

The Japanese word that corresponds to English **Mr.**, **Mrs.**, **Miss**, and **Ms.** is *san*. The Japanese always use *san* (or other, more formal titles of respect) with proper names. Even among family members or close personal friends who use first names with each other, *san* follows the name.

Be sure to use *san* in direct address (when speaking directly to someone), and when referring to someone else. *Never* use *san* to refer to yourself.

EXAMPLES

Tanaka san, kōhī wa ikaga desu ka. / **Mr. Tanaka, would you like some coffee?**

Merī san wa, kyō gakkō ni imasu ka. / **Is Mary at school today?**

But note the following:

Watakushi wa, John Smith desu. / **I'm John Smith.**

§4.7 POLITENESS

The prefix *o-* before certain nouns expresses *politeness*. (This is also used with verbs and adjectives. See §7 and §8.)

EXAMPLES

namae, onamae / **name**

kane, okane / **money**

sake, osake / **rice wine**

furo, ofuro / **bath**

hashi, ohashi / **chopsticks**

tegami, otegami / **letter**

A variation of this form is *go-*, which is used with words of Chinese origin.

hon, gohon / **book**

kekkon, gokekkon / **marriage**

Note the following about the prefixes *o-* and *go-*:

- Although both men and women may use the above forms, in some cases, these prefixes would be used only by women, as in the "o" forms in examples below.

EXAMPLES

    niku, oniku / **meat**   yasai, oyasai / **vegetables**

- Some words are *always* used with the polite prefix. The *o-* and *go-* are now part of the words:

EXAMPLES

    ocha / **Japanese tea**   gohan / **cooked rice, food**

- These prefixes cannot be used with all nouns. It's best to use them only when you are certain they are correct, as with the examples above.

§4.8 COMPOUND NOUNS

When two nouns are used together to make a *compound* noun, they are usually joined by the particle *no*.

EXAMPLES

    rekishi no kurasu / **history class**

    eigo no sensei / **English teacher**

    apāto no biru / **apartment building**

    Some compound nouns may be formed *without* the *no*, however.

EXAMPLES

    kōhī jawan / **coffee cup**

    kankō basu / **tour bus**

    bōeki gaisha / **trading company**

§4.9 NOUN SUFFIXES

- The suffix -ya, when added to a noun, means the place or shop where that thing is sold, or the person or shopkeeper who sells it.

  EXAMPLES

  niku / **meat** ──────────▶ nikuya / **butcher shop, butcher**

  hon / **book** ──────────▶ honya / **bookstore, clerk, owner**

  kamera / **camera** ──────────▶ kameraya / **camera shop, clerk, owner**

- When referring to the clerk or shopkeeper, the title *san* is used:

  EXAMPLES

  nikuya san / **butcher**

  kameraya san / **camera shop clerk**

- The suffix -ka, when added to a noun, means a person with expertise or special knowledge on that subject.

  EXAMPLES

  seiji / **politics** ──────────▶ seijika / **politician**

  hyoron / **commentary** ──────────▶ hyoronka / **critic**

  shosetsu / **novel** ──────────▶ shosetsuka / **novelist**

  geijutsu / **art** ──────────▶ geijutsuka / **artist**

§5.

Pronouns

§5.1 WHAT ARE PRONOUNS?

A *pronoun* is a word that takes the place of a noun. Here are some common English pronouns: **I, you, he, she, it, we, they**. These are personal pronouns used as *subjects*. Other common English pronouns are **me, him, her, us, them**. These are personal pronouns used as *objects*. **You** and it, of course, may be subjects or objects. In addition to these, there are other kinds of pronouns, such as *possessive* (**mine, yours, his**, etc.), *demonstrative* (**this, that**), and *interrogative* (**who, where, what**, etc.)

Japanese pronoun usage is quite different from that of English, as you will see from the following discussion.

§5.2 PERSONAL PRONOUNS

Personal pronouns in Japanese refer to people, not things or ideas. Japanese has no equivalent to the English **it** in this category.

When the meaning can be understood from the context, the Japanese prefer *not* to use personal pronouns. Use these with care, and be sure to read the information that follows.

29

Singular	Plural
watakushi / **I, me**	watakushitachi / **we, us**
anata / **you**	anatatachi / **you** anatagata / **you** (polite)
kare / **he, him**	karera / **they, them** (all male or male and female)
kanojo / **she, her**	kanojotachi / **they, them** (female) kanojora / **they, them** (female)

§5.2-1 Special Usage

anata / **you**

Avoid using this whenever possible. In speaking to someone directly, try to use the person's name and *san* instead.

EXAMPLE

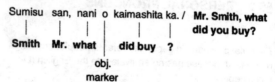

When speaking to a teacher, a doctor, a dentist, or a member of the Diet (the Japanese legislature), use the word *sensei*, either alone, or after the person's last name. *Sensei*, which literally means "teacher," may also be used with others not listed above. A teacher can be one who has achieved success or earned respect in his or her field.

You can use *sensei*, for example, to address an artist, writer, architect, musician, or other talented person.

EXAMPLE

Sensei, ogenki desu ka. / **Sir (teacher), how have you been?**

If you are speaking to a group, you can use the following expressions for "you" (plural):

EXAMPLE

mina san / **everyone (you all)**   mina sama / **everyone (you all)**

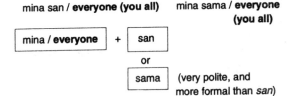

mina / **everyone** + san

or

sama (very polite, and more formal than *san*)

EXAMPLES

Mina san, ohayō gozaimasu. / **Good morning, everyone.**

Mina sama, sayōnara. / **Goodbye, everyone!**

kare / **he**   kanojo / **she**

• Whenever possible, when referring to a third person, use the person's name.

EXAMPLE

Sumisu san wa Nyūyōku kara kimashita ka. / **Is Mrs. Smith from New York?**

This is better than saying, "Is *she* from New York?" Of course, if it is clear who the subject is, it can be left out entirely.

- Several other terms can be used instead of the pronouns *kare*, *kanojo*, and their plural forms. The Japanese prefer these:

Singular	Plural
ano hito / **that person**	ano hitotachi / **those persons**
ano kata / **that person (polite)**	ano katagata / **those persons (polite)**

EXAMPLES

Kinō | ano hito | ni aimashita ka. / **Did you see him (that person) yesterday?**

that person

| Ano katagata | wa kinō irasshaimashita. / **They (those persons) were here yesterday.**

those persons

§5.2-2 Case

Case refers to the form of a pronoun which shows its relationship to other words in a sentence.

In English, the personal pronouns have three cases: the *nominative* (used for the subject of a sentence or clause), the *objective* (used for the object of a sentence, indirect object, or object of a preposition), and the *possessive* (showing ownership). English has a different set of personal pronouns for each of these cases.

EXAMPLES

He lives here.	*He* = nominative case (subject of the sentence)
I see *him*.	*him* = objective case (object of the verb)
His car is here.	*His* = possessive case (shows ownership)

In Japanese, the personal pronouns function with all three cases, but the words stay the same. The case is shown by a *particle*, or postposition, that comes after the pronoun. Note that in the following examples of how one pronoun, *watakushi*, is used for different grammatical functions, the topic marker *wa*, rather than the subject marker *ga*, is preferred. This will be discussed in more detail in the chapter on Particles (see §6).

EXAMPLES

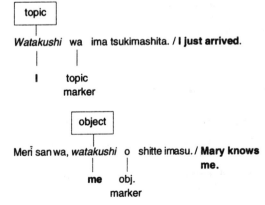

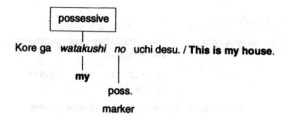

Kore ga *watakushi no* uchi desu. / **This is my house**.

my — poss. marker

§5.3 INTERROGATIVE PRONOUNS

dare / **who**
dō / **how**
doko / **where** (place)
donna / **what kind of**
dochira / **where, which** (direction, preference)
dore / **which** (persons, things)
donata / **which person** (polite)
dōshite / **why**
nan, nani / **what**
nannin / **how many people**
ikura / **how much**
ikutsu / **how many**
itsu / **when**

§5.4 INDEFINITE PRONOUNS

dareka / **someone**	daremo / **no one**
donataka / **someone** (polite)	donatamo / **no one** (polite)
doreka / **something**	doremo / **nothing**

dokoka / **somewhere**	dokomo / **nowhere**
nanika / **something**	nanimo / **nothing**
ikuraka / **some, a little**	ikuramo / **not much**
nandemo / **anything**	nannimo / **nothing**

Note that the expressions listed on the right side of the preceding chart take *negative* verbs in order to have a negative meaning.

EXAMPLES

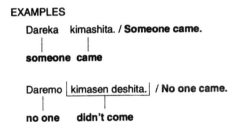

Dareka   kimashita. / **Someone came.**

someone came

Daremo | kimasen deshita. | / **No one came.**

no one   didn't come

§5.5 DEMONSTRATIVE PRONOUNS

The *demonstrative* words (some are pronouns and some are adjectives) form a pattern of prefixes:

ko- / **here** (close to the speaker)
so- / **there** (away from the speaker)
a- / **over there** (some distance from the speaker)
do- / **question**

The last one, *do-*, can be seen in **§5.4** above.

Here are the rest:

	ko- / **here**	so- / **there**	a- / **over there**
Pronoun	kore / **this**	sore / **that**	are / **that**
Adjective	kono / **this**	sono / **that**	ano / **that**
Adjective	konna / **this kind of**	sonna / **that kind of**	anna / **that kind of**
Adverb	kō / **in this manner**	sō / **in that manner**	ā / **in that manner**
Adverb, Pronoun	koko / **here**	soko / **there**	asoko / **over there**
Adverb, Pronoun	kochira / **here, this**	sochira / **there, that**	achira / **there, that**

§5.6   RELATIVE PRONOUNS

The *relative* pronouns in English are **who, whom, whose, which, where,** and **that.** Because relative clauses in Japanese precede, rather than follow, the words they modify, Japanese does not have words that correspond to these pronouns.

EXAMPLE

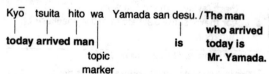

Kyō	tsuita	hito	wa	Yamada san desu.	**The man who arrived today is Mr. Yamada.**
today	**arrived**	**man**	topic marker	**is**	

Notice that the Japanese sentence has no word to correspond to the relative pronoun "who" in the English sentences.

This will be explained further in the section on Verbs (see **§7**).

§5.7 REFLEXIVE PRONOUNS

The *reflexive* pronouns in English are words such as **myself, yourself, himself, yourselves**, and so forth. Japanese has only one word to correspond to these pronouns. You might call it an all-purpose reflexive pronoun. Its meaning is both singular and plural, masculine and feminine. It can be used for humans and for warm-blooded animals. It cannot be used for fish, reptiles, insects, or inanimate objects.

> jibun / **one's self**

This is commonly followed by particles such as *de* or *no* (see **§6**).

EXAMPLES

Jibun de ikimasu. / **I'm going myself.**

Jibun de shinasai. / **Do it yourself.**

Jibun no koto wa jibun de shinasai. / **Do your own work by yourself.**

Merī san wa, jibun de benkyō shite imasu. / **Mary is studying by herself.**

§6.

Particles

§6.1 WHAT ARE PARTICLES?

A particle is a word that shows the relationship of a word,
a phrase, or a clause to the rest of the sentence. Some
particles show grammatical function–subject, object,
indirect object. Some have meaning themselves, like
English prepositions. But since they always *follow* the
word or words they mark, they are *post*positions.

The lists that follow include some of the more common
particles, and some of their uses.

§6.2 PARTICLES USED WITH WORDS OR PHRASES

wa	de	made ni
ga	e	mo
o	hodo	shika
no	ka	to
ni	kara	ya
dake	made	yori

wa

topic marker

How do you decide if an expression is a topic, marked with *wa*, or a subject, marked with *ga*? Both look like the subject of an English sentence!

Think of the topic as a comment on something that has already been introduced into the conversation, or that is part of general or shared knowledge. As such, *wa* can mean

"Speaking of (the) . . ." or "As for (the)."

EXAMPLES

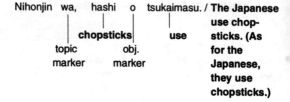

Kimura san wa, gakusei desu. / **Mr. Kimura is a student. (Speaking of Mr. Kimura, he's a student.)**

topic marker **student** **is**

Nihonjin wa, hashi o tsukaimasu. / **The Japanese use chopsticks. (As for the Japanese, they use chopsticks.)**

topic marker **chopsticks** obj. marker **use**

contrast

Wa can follow a noun to show contrast. The thing being contrasted may or may not be stated, but with this usage, contrast is implied.

EXAMPLES

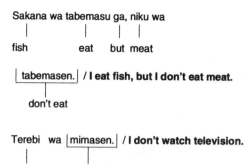

Sakana wa tabemasu ga, niku wa

fish   eat   but meat

| tabemasen. | / **I eat fish, but I don't eat meat.**

don't eat

Terebi wa | mimasen. | / **I don't watch television.**

Television don't watch

ga

subject marker

Ga marks what the Japanese call the grammatical *subject* of
a sentence. Think of the subject in the following two ways:

• First, in neutral descriptions of observable actions or
situations.

EXAMPLES

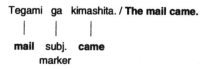

Tegami ga kimashita. / **The mail came.**

mail subj. came
marker

Ame ga | hutte imasu. | / **It's raining. (The rain is**
  | | **falling.)**
rain subj.   **is falling**
    marker

Note that in the negative counterparts of these sentences, *wa*, not *ga*, must be used.

Tegami wa kimasen deshita. / **The mail didn't come.**

- Second, for special emphasis, to distinguish a particular person or thing from all others.

EXAMPLES

Watakushi ga shimashita. / **I did it. (I am the one who did it.)**

Tōkyō ga ōkii desu. / **Tokyo is big. (It is Tokyo that is big.)**

- When an interrogative pronoun is used as the subject of a sentence, *ga* must always be used too.

EXAMPLE

Dare ga, kore o shimashita ka. / **Who did this?**
   | | | | | | **(Who is the one**
who subj. **this** obj.   did   ?   **who did this?)**
    marker   marker

---

object marker

O usually marks the object. But *ga* marks the object of certain non-action verbs and certain adjectives and adjectival nouns (see **§8**.)

EXAMPLES

Yōko   san   wa,   eigo   ga   wakarimasu. / **Yoko
                                                under-
         topic   **English** obj. **understands**   stands
         marker   marker   English.**

Nihongo   ga | dekimasu ka. | / **Can you speak
                                       Japanese?**
             obj.   **can do ?**
           marker

Hon   ga   hoshii desu. / **I want a book.**
 | | |
book obj. **want**
        marker

Merī   san   wa,   tenisu   ga   jōzu   desu. / **Mary is good
                                                    at tennis.**
              topic   obj. **good at** **is**
              marker   marker

| o |

| direct object marker |

EXAMPLES

Senshū   sono   hon   o   yomimashita. / **I read that
                                               book last
last week **that** **book**   **read**   week.**

Jon san wa eiga o mimashita. / **John saw a movie.**

| | |
| movie | saw |

through, along, in

The particle *o* is used with verbs such as **walk**, **run**, **drive**, **go through**, etc., when speaking of continuous motion and a finite place or distance.

EXAMPLES

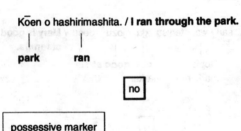

Tanaka san wa, Gobangai o arukimashita. / **Mr. Tanaka walked along Fifth Avenue.**

| | |
| Fifth Avenue | walked |

Kōen o hashirimashita. / **I ran through the park.**

| | |
| park | ran |

no

possessive marker

Think of this like the English apostrophe plus **s**.

EXAMPLES

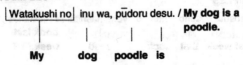

Watakushi no inu wa, pūdoru desu. / **My dog is a poodle.**

| | | | |
| My | dog | poodle | is |

| Kodomo no | kao ga yogorete imasu. / **The child's face** |
| | **is dirty.** |

Child's   face   dirty   is

---

noun modification

This usage of *no* is similar to the possessive, but it is seen more with compound nouns or noun phrases.

EXAMPLES

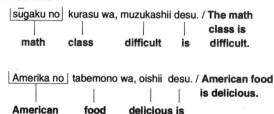

sūgaku no	kurasu wa, muzukashii desu. / **The math**
	class is
	difficult.

math   class   difficult   is

| Amerika no | tabemono wa, oishii desu. / **American food** |
| | **is delicious.** |

American   food   delicious is

---

appositional

No links the noun or pronoun to the appositive that follows.

EXAMPLES

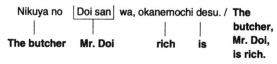

Nikuya no | Doi san | wa, okanemochi desu. / **The**
                                               butcher,
                                             Mr. Doi,
                                             is rich.

The butcher   Mr. Doi   rich   is

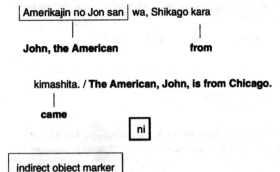

Amerikajin no Jon san | wa, Shikago kara
└──────────┬──────────┘   └──┬──┘
John, the American   from

kimashita. / **The American, John, is from Chicago.**
    │
  came

ni

indirect object marker

EXAMPLES

Yamada san ni hanashimashita. / **I talked to Ms.**
         │   │   **Yamada.**
        to   talked

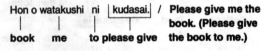

Hon o watakushi ni | kudasai. | / **Please give me the**
  │   │   │   │   **book. (Please give**
 book   me   to   please give   **the book to me.)**

- Note that some Japanese verbs, such as **ask** and **meet**,
  take an indirect object, although their English counterparts
  do not.

EXAMPLES

Watakushi wa, Tanaka san ni kikimashita. / **I asked Mr.**
                      │   │   **Tanaka.**
                     to   asked

Tomodachi ni aimashita. / **I met my friend.**
    │   │   │
 friend   to   met

location

With stative (non-action) verbs meaning **there is/are**, *imasu* for people, *arimasu* for things, *ni* means **in**, **at**, or **on**, and so forth.

EXAMPLES

Merī san wa, Kyōto ni imasu. / **Mary is in Kyoto.**

Ginza wa Tōkyō ni arimasu. / **Ginza is in Tokyo.**

Haha wa depāto ni imasu. / **My mother is at the department store.**

| | |
my   department
mother   store

For location, the equivalents of English expressions **near**, **under**, **inside**, **on top of**, etc. are useful. Note how they are formed in Japanese. First look at the following words:

ue / **top**	shita / **bottom**
mae / **front**	ushiro / **back**
naka / **inside**	soto / **outside**
chikaku / **nearby**	tonari / **next to**

These words are nouns in Japanese. To form a locational phrase, the particle *no* links another noun to one of these, and then the particle *ni* follows.

tēburu no ue ni / **on top of the table**

table   's top on

Hon wa, tēburu no ue ni arimasu. / **The book is on top of the table.**

uchi   no   naka   ni / **inside the house**

| | | |

house 's inside in

Jon san wa, uchi no naka ni imasu. / **John is inside the house.**

eki   no   chikaku   ni / **near the station**

| | | |

station 's   nearby   at

Yubinkyoku wa, eki no chikaku ni arimasu. / **The post office is near the station.**

---

direction

With verbs of motion, *ni* means **to** or **toward**.

EXAMPLES

Nakamura san wa, | mainichi | Tōkyō

every day

ni ikimasu. / **Mrs. Nakamura goes to Tokyo every day.**

| |

to goes

| Ano hito | wa, Amerika ni kaerimashita. / **He returned to**
| | | | **America.**
He | | **to** | **returned**

specific time

With expressions of specific time, *ni* means **at** (clock time), **in** (month, year), or **on** (day).

EXAMPLES

> ichiji ni / **at one o'clock**
> gogo juichiji ni / **at 11 P.M.**

| Ano hitotachi | wa, | shichiji han | ni tsukimashita. / **They**
| | | | | **arrived**
They | | **7:30** | **at** | **arrived** | **at 7:30.**

> rokugatsu ni / **in June**
> kugatsu ni / **in September**
> senkyuhyakukyuju nen ni / **in (the year) 1990**

Ano hito wa, shigatsu ni | umaremashita. | / **He was**
| | | **born in**
April | **in** | **was born** | **April.**

Watakushi wa, 1991 nen ni Nihon ni
                 | | | |
              year in Japan to

ikimashita. / **I went to Japan in 1991.**
  |
went

> getsuyōbi ni / **on Monday**
> kinyobi ni / **on Friday**

Getsuyōbi ni shigoto o hajimemasu. / **I begin work on**
    | | | | **Monday.**
Monday on work   begin

Kayōbi ni sore o shimashō. / **Let's do it on Tuesday.**
  | | | |
Tuesday on it   let's do

---

notion of per

Ni, is used with expressions such as **per hour**, **per day**, **per person**, etc.

EXAMPLES

ichijikan ni san doru / **three dollars per hour**
   | | | |
hour per three dollars

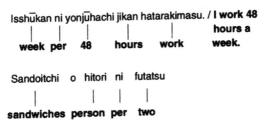

Isshūkan ni yonjūhachi jikan hatarakimasu. / **I work 48 hours a week.**

week per 48 hours work

Sandoitchi o hitori ni futatsu

sandwiches person per two

tsukurimasu. / **I'll make two sandwiches per person.**

will make

For some other uses of *ni*, see §7.12 and §7.13.

> dake

> limitation

Dake translates English words such as **only, all, just, no more than, as many as,** and **as much as.**

EXAMPLES

Sore dake desu ka. / **Is that all?**

that all is ?

Terebi wa, nyūsu bangumi dake mimasu. / **On television I watch only the news.**

news program only watch

Suki na　dake　tabete　kudasai. / **Please eat as much**
　|　　|　　|　　　|　　　　　　　**as you want.**

want　as much as　eat　please

place of action

This use of *de* means **in, at, on,** and so forth. It is used with action verbs, not stative verbs or verbs showing existence.

EXAMPLE

Panya　de　kaimashita. / **I bought it at the bakery.**
　|　　|　　　|

bakery　at　　bought

means

De translates **by,** or **by means of, with, in,** etc.

EXAMPLES

Takushī　de　ikimashita. / **I went by taxi.**
　|　　　|　　|

taxi　by　went

Jisho　de　shirabemashita. / **I checked it in the**
　|　　|　　　|　　　　　　　　　　**dictionary.**

dictionary　in　　checked

---

totalizing

This use of *de* connotes a **unit**, a **certain number** or
amount, or **together**.

EXAMPLES

futari de / **(by) two people**

Futari de shimasu. / **Two of us (together) will do it.**

will do

Nihon ni | futari de| ikimasu. / **Two of us will go**
                                             to Japan.
Japan to two people will go

| Zenbu de| sen en desu. / **All together it's 1,000 yen.**

all together 1,000 yen is

---

time limit

The meaning of *de* here is **within** or **in** for a given length of
time.

EXAMPLES

Nishūkan de |dekimasu.| / **I can do it within two**
                                           weeks.

two weeks within can do

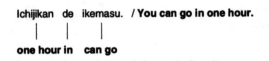

Ichijikan de ikemasu. / **You can go in one hour.**

one hour in can go

| scope |

Here *de* means **among, of, within**, etc., referring to extent or range.

EXAMPLES

Kudamono de, nani ga ichiban suki

fruit of which most like

desu ka. / **Which of the fruit do you like the most?**

is ?

Amerika de, doko ni | ikitai desu | ka. / **Where in America do you want to go?**

within where want to go ?

| material |

Here *de* means **of** or **from** in **made of** or **made from** expressions.

EXAMPLES

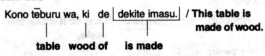

Kono tēburu wa, ki de | dekite imasu. | / **This table is made of wood.**

table wood of is made

Kore wa, gin de tsukurimashita. / **I made it of silver.**

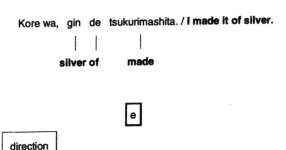

silver of   made

e

direction

Like *ni*, *e* is used with verbs of motion to indicate **to** or **toward**.

EXAMPLE

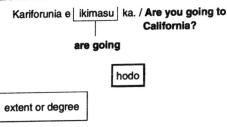

Kariforunia e | ikimasu | ka. / **Are you going to California?**

are going

hodo

extent or degree

Hodo means **as much as**, or **as . . . as**, and it is often used in negative constructions, although the meaning is positive.

EXAMPLES

Watakushi wa, anata hodo

I   you as much as

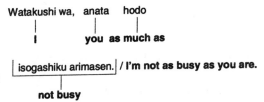

| isogashiku arimasen. | / **I'm not as busy as you are.**

not busy

Kore hodo oishii mono wa arimasen. / **There's nothing as delicious as this.**

| | | | |
| this | delicious thing | | |

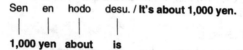

about, approximately

With things that can be counted, *hodo* means **about** or **approximately**.

EXAMPLES

Sen en hodo desu. / **It's about 1,000 yen.**

| | | | |
| **1,000 yen** | **about** | **is** | |

Isshūkan hodo de | dekimasu. | / **It can be done in about a week.**

| | | | |
| **a week** | **about** | **in** | **can be done** |

ka

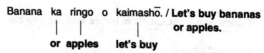

enumerative

The meaning of *ka* here is **or**, that is, listing parallel things and then choosing.

EXAMPLES

Banana ka ringo o kaimashō. / **Let's buy bananas or apples.**

| | | | |
| | **or apples** | **let's buy** | |

Kōhī ka, kōcha ka, kokoa wa
coffee or tea or cocoa

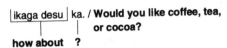

ikaga desu ka. / **Would you like coffee, tea,**
or cocoa?
how about ?

Note that *ka*, like many particles, has several meanings. In
the example above, it is also used as the question marker at
the end of the sentence.

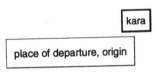

kara

place of departure, origin

The meaning of *kara* here is **from**.

EXAMPLES

Kono kisha wa, Kyōto kara kimashita. / **This train**
came from
this train from came **Kyoto.**

Watakushi wa, Nihon kara kimashita. / **I am from Japan.**

I from

starting time

The meaning of *kara* here would be expressed by **at** in
English, but in Japanese, the meaning is **from a certain**
time and continuing on. In other words, it is the beginning

of a period of time. It differs from the use of the particle *ni*, which means **at a precise time,** (**Meet me at one o'clock.**)

EXAMPLES

Gēmu wa, ichiji kara hajimarimasu. / **The game**
| | | **begins**

game   **one o'clock from**   **begins**   **at one o'clock.**

Getsuyōbi kara isogashiku narimasu. / **Starting**
| | | **Monday, I'll**

Monday from   **busy**   **become**   **be busy.**

| source |

Kara also means **from** in the sense of **origin.**

EXAMPLES

Tanaka san kara kikimashita. / **I heard it from Mrs.**
                          Tanaka.

      from   **heard**

Kono hon wa, toshokan kara karimashita. / **I borrowed**
| | | | **this book**

this book   **library**   **from borrowed**   **from the library.**

made

target time or place

Made means **until, as far as.** It is often combined with *kara* in a sentence.

EXAMPLES

Yūgata made | benkyō shimashita. | / **I studied until**
| | | **evening.**
evening until   studied

Tsugi no kado | made | | arukimashō. | / **Let's walk as**
| | | **far as the next**
next   corner as far as let's walk   corner.

Gakkō wa, kuji kara sanji made
| | | |
school 9 o'clock from 3 o'clock until

desu. / **School is from 9 until 3 o'clock.**
|
is

made ni

time limit

Unlike the time limit usage of the particle *de* (**within**), *made ni* means **by** (the time given), or **not later than.**

EXAMPLES

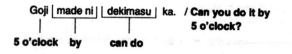

Goji | made ni | dekimasu | ka. / **Can you do it by 5 o'clock?**

5 o'clock   by   can do

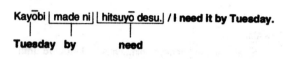

Kayōbi | made ni | hitsuyō desu. | / **I need it by Tuesday.**

Tuesday by   need

mo

including, excluding

Mo means **also** or **too**. Depending on which word it follows in a sentence, *mo* can replace *wa*, *ga*, or *o*. When used with a negative verb, The meaning is **(not) either**, or **neither . . . nor**.

EXAMPLES

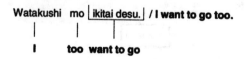

Watakushi | mo | ikitai desu. | / **I want to go too.**

I   too want to go

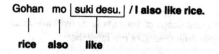

Gohan | mo | suki desu. | / **I also like rice.**

rice also like

Yōko san wa, niku mo sakana mo
| | | |
meat neither fish nor

| tabemasen. | / **Yoko eats neither meat nor fish.**
|
doesn't eat

emphasis

This meaning of *mo* is **even** in the sense of emphasis.

EXAMPLES

Ano Amerikajin wa, sashimi mo
| |
raw fish even

tabemasu. / **That American even eats raw fish.**
|
eats

Ichi doru mo | arimasen. | / **I don't even have one**
| | | | **dollar.**
one dollar even there isn't

shika

limitation

Shika means **only, just.** Although the meaning is affirmative, it takes the negative form of the verb.

EXAMPLES

Eigo   shika   shirimasen. / **I only know English.**
| | |
English only   don't know

Shinbun   shika   yomimasen. / **I only read newspapers.**
| | |
newspapers only   don't read

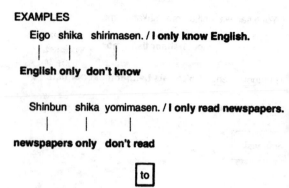

to

complete listing

To means **and** when stating all possible items in a list. The implication is **and nothing more.**

EXAMPLES

Jon san to Meri san ga kimashita. / **John and Mary**
                                          came.

Enpitsu to,   nōto   to,   jōgi o
| | | |
pencils and notebook and ruler

   kaimashita. / **I bought pencils, a notebook, and**
        | **a ruler.**
   bought

involvement

Here, *to* means **together with.**

EXAMPLES

Satō san to   honya   e   ikimashita. / **I went to the**
           | | | | **bookstore**
     with bookstore to went with Mr. Sato.

Tom san to   issho ni hon o kakimashita. / **I wrote**
         | | | | **a book**
   with together book wrote   with Tom.

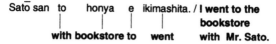

quotation

To follows both direct and indirect quotations.

EXAMPLES

Ono san wa, "Watakushi ga | shimasu |,"
              | |
            I   **will do**

to iimashita. / **"I'll do it," said Mr. Ono.**
|
said

Ono san wa, kare ga suru to iimashita. / **Mr. Ono said**
             | | | **that he**
           he   would do said   would do it.

ya

partial listing

Ya is used for **and** when stating a sample of, or some of the
items in, a list. The implication is **and others, among**

others, or **such things as;** that is, something has been left out.

EXAMPLES

Jon san ya Meri san ga kimashita. / **John and Mary came.**

Enpitsu ya, nōto ya, jōgi o
pencil and notebook and ruler

kaimashita. / **I bought a pencil, a notebook, and**
bought **a ruler.**

yori

comparison

Used when comparing things, *yori* means **than.** Think of it as the **than** in expressions such as **bigger than, smaller than, better than, worse than, rather than,** etc. It is often used in combination with *hō* (contrast) (see §8.)

EXAMPLES

Kore yori sore o kudasai. / **Please give me that**
rather than this.
this rather than that please give

Pan yori gohan no hō ga
bread more than rice

suki desu. / **I like rice more than bread.**
like

Kyōto wa, Tōkyō yori samui desu. / **Kyoto is colder**
            | | | **than Tokyo.**

          more than cold is

Amerika wa, Nihon yori ōkii desu. / **America is**
         | | | **larger than**
        more than large is **Japan.**

§6.3 PARTICLES USED WITH CLAUSES

ga	node
kara	noni
keredo	to
nagara	

| ga |

| contrary reasoning |

Ga means **but**, or **although**. The implication is **despite the circumstances**.

EXAMPLES

Samui desu ga, dekakemashita. / **Although it's cold,**
  | | | | **I went out.**
cold is although went out

Byōki desu ga, shigoto ni ikimasu. / **I'm sick, but I'm**
  | | | | | | **going to work.**
sick am but   work to go

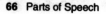

neutral connector

Here, *ga* means **and**.

EXAMPLES

Hawai ni ikimashita ga, | subarashikatta desu. |/ **I went to**
 | | | | **Hawaii,**
 went **and** **wonderful was** **and it was**
 wonderful.

Sono hon o yomimashita ga,
 | |
 read **and**

| omoshirokatta desu. |/ **I read that book, and it was**
 | **interesting.**
 was interesting

kara

reason

Here, *kara* means **because** or **since**.

EXAMPLES

Isogashii kara ikemasen. / **Because I'm busy, I**
 | | | **can't go.**
 busy **because** **can't go**

Ame da kara uchi ni imasu. / **Since it's raining, I'll**
 | | | | | | **stay home.**
 rain **is** **since** **home** **at** **stay**

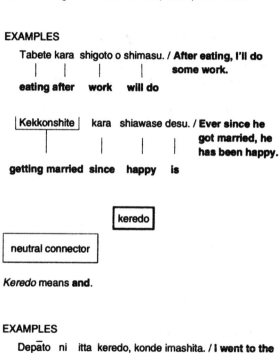

sequential action

The meaning of *kara* here is **after, since, ever since.**

EXAMPLES

Tabete kara shigoto o shimasu. / **After eating, I'll do**
|　　　　|　　　　|　　　|　　　　**some work.**
eating after　　work　　will do

| Kekkonshite | kara shiawase desu. / **Ever since he**
　　　|　　　　　　|　　　|　　|　　　　**got married, he**
　　　　　　　　　　　　　　　　　　　　　has been happy.
getting married since　happy　is

keredo

neutral connector

Keredo means **and.**

EXAMPLES

Depāto　ni　itta keredo, konde imashita. / **I went to the**
|　　　|　　|　　|　　　|　　　　　|　　　　**department**
department to went and crowded was　　store, and
store　　　　　　　　　　　　　　　　　　　　it was
**　　　　　　　　　　　　　　　　　　　　　　crowded.**

Takushī ni notta keredo, | takakatta desu. | / I took a taxi,
　　|　　|　　|　　|　　　　　　|　　　　　and it was
　　taxi　on　got　and　　was expensive　expensive.

contrary reasoning

Here, *keredo* means **but, although, however**.

EXAMPLES

Yonda keredo, | wakarimasen deshita. | / I read it, but I
　|　　|　　　　　　|　　　　　　　　　　　　didn't under-
　read　but　　didn't understand　　　　stand it.

Eiga wa omoshirokatta　keredo,
　|　　　　　|　　　　　　|
movie was interesting although

| nete shimaimashita. | / **Although the movie was**
　　　　　　　　　　　　　　interesting, I fell asleep.
　　fell asleep

nagara

simultaneous action

Nagara means **while** or **as**.

EXAMPLES

Aruki　nagara, hanashimashita. / **While walking, we**
　|　　　　|　　　　　　|　　　　　　　　**talked.**
walking while　　talked

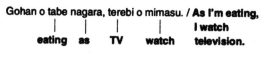

Gohan o tabe nagara, terebi o mimasu. / **As I'm eating,**
      | | | | **I watch**
  eating **as**   **TV** **watch** **television.**

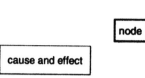

| node |

| cause and effect |

Node means **since** or **because** when followed by an "effect" clause.

EXAMPLES

Kumotte iru node, umi ni |ikimasen.| / **Since it's**
    | | | | **cloudy, I'm**
cloudy **is since beach to not going** **not going to**
                         the beach.

Hashitta node, |tsukaremashita.| / **Because I ran, I got**
   | | | **tired.**
ran because   **got tired**

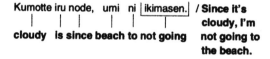

| noni |

| contrast |

Noni means **in spite of** or **although**, with contrast between the two clauses implied.

EXAMPLES

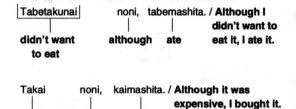

Tabetakunai noni, tabemashita. / **Although I didn't want to eat it, I ate it.**

didn't want to eat   although   ate

Takai noni, kaimashita. / **Although it was expensive, I bought it.**

expensive   although   bought

| to |

| condition |

When discussing under what condition, or under which circumstance, *to* means **if** or **when**.

EXAMPLES

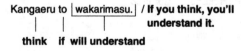

Kangaeru to wakarimasu. / **If you think, you'll understand it.**

think   if   will understand

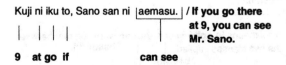

Kuji ni iku to, Sano san ni aemasu. / **If you go there at 9, you can see Mr. Sano.**

9   at   go   if   can see

Tōkyō ni tsuku   to, ame ga futte imashita. / **When I**
  | | | | | **arrived**
arrived when rain falling was   **in Tokyo,**
it was
raining.

§6.4 PARTICLES USED WITH SENTENCES

The following particles are used at the end of sentences.

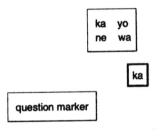

ka	yo
ne	wa

ka

question marker

Ka is like the English question mark at the end of a
sentence. In Japanese, however, the word order of a
statement does not change when a question is formed.

EXAMPLES

Horiguchi san wa, kirei desu. / **Mrs. Horiguchi is**
              | | **beautiful.**
             beautiful is

Horiguchi san wa, kirei desu ka. / **Is Mrs. Horiguchi beautiful?**

is ?

Imōto san wa, sensei desu ka. / **Is your sister a teacher?**

sister　　　　teacher　is ?

Doko de | ban gohan | o | tabetai desu | ka. / **Where do you want to eat dinner?**

where　　dinner　　　　want to eat　?

Itsu　eigo　o | benkyō shimashita | ka. / **When did you study English?**

when English　　　studied　　　　　?

ne

confirmation

Ne is similar to the English tag questions **don't you think so,** or **isn't it?** It calls for the listener to agree with or confirm what the speaker has said.

EXAMPLES

Atsui desu | ne. | / **It's hot, isn't it?**
   | | |
hot   is isn't it

Omoshiroi eiga deshita | ne. | / **It was a good movie,**
                                       wasn't it?
good movie was wasn't it

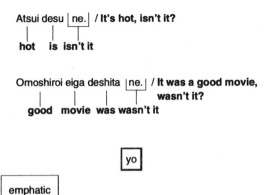

yo

emphatic

One usage of *yo* is similar to the English exclamation point.
In that sense, it conveys emotion or strong feeling. It can
also be an expression of emphasis, such as **I'm certain** (of
what has just been said). Because men and women use *yo*
differently, and because it can be assertive, beginners
should use it with care.

EXAMPLES

| Benkyō shinasai | yo. / **Study!**
     |
   study

Fujisan wa, kirei   desu yo. / **Mt. Fuji is beautiful!**
   | | | |
Mt. Fuji beautiful is !

| wa |

| female sentence ending |

Used only by women, *wa* doesn't translate easily. It can have both an emphatic function and a softening effect.

EXAMPLES

Totemo atsui wa. / **It's very hot.**
| |
very   hot

Watakushi ga suru wa. / **I'll do it.**
|
will do

§7.

Verbs

§7.1 WHAT ARE VERBS?

Verbs are words that describe an action, a process, or a state of being.

Verbs have different forms which enable you to express time, intention, feelings, politeness, etc. Japanese verbs express these things too, but in different ways from those of English and other Indo-European languages. As you have seen in §3, for example, the main verb of a Japanese sentence must be at the end. In this section, you will see other differences, as well as some similarities.

§7.2 AGREEMENT

In English a verb must agree with its subject in person and number. In the present tense, for example, a subject in the first person takes a different verb form from a subject in the third person. And a plural subject in the third person takes a different verb form from a singular subject.

EXAMPLE

Person	Singular	Plural
First Person	**I go**	**we go**
Second Person	**you go**	**you go**
Third Person	**he/she/it goes**	**they go**

- In Japanese, agreement is not an issue. Verbs do not have different forms to indicate person, number, or gender. The *same* verb form is used no matter what the subject. This is true for all tenses.

EXAMPLE

Person	Singular	Plural
First Person	ikimasu / **I go**	ikimasu / **we go**
Second Person	ikimasu / **you go**	ikimasu / **you go**
Third Person	ikimasu / **he /she/it goes**	ikimasu / **they go**

- This principle is easy to understand if you remember that, if the meaning is clear from the context in a Japanese sentence, a pronoun is not necessary. Therefore, *Ikimasu* is both a verb and a sentence.

- In English, except for the imperative, or command form, a sentence consisting of a verb alone is not possible.

§7.3 VERB CONJUGATIONS

Japanese verbs can be classified into two major groups, or conjugations. The only exceptions are two irregular verbs: *suru*, **to do,** and *kuru*, **to come.**

These groupings are a basic key to the Japanese verb system. They enable you to change the verb forms for different tenses and moods.

In a dictionary, an English verb is listed in its infinitive, or **to** form: **(to) go**, **(to) see**, etc. A Japanese verb, on the other hand, is listed in what is called its "dictionary form." The dictionary form is the basis for categorizing a verb into one of the two major conjugations.

The two groups differ in how they form their stems and their infinitives. The stem is the most important inflectional base, which may change, or to which different suffixes, or endings, are added, to show tense, mood, and politeness level. The infinitive is the second most important inflectional base.

§7.3-1 The Consonant Conjugation

In this group, the verb stems end in a consonant. Therefore, they may be called **c-stem** verbs, as we shall do here. Because the stems are formed by dropping the final **u**, this is also referred to as the **u-dropping conjugation**, and the verbs may be called **u-dropping verbs**.

How can you tell a Consonant Conjugation verb?

If the dictionary form ends in anything but *-eru* or *-iru*, it belongs in this group.

How do you form the stem?

To form the stem of the verb, drop the final *-u*.

EXAMPLES

DICTIONARY FORM	STEM	ENGLISH
isogu	isog-	to hurry
kaku	kak-	to write
nuru	nur-	to paint
tobu	tob-	to fly
shinu	shin-	to die
yomu	yom-	to read

- For a few verbs, certain sound changes are necessary:

  If a verb ends in -*su*, the stem ends in *sh* before a suffix beginning with *i*, or *s* before other suffixes.

  If a verb ends in -*tsu*, the stem ends in *ch* before a suffix beginning with *i*, or *t* before other suffixes. For example:

DICTIONARY FORM	STEM	ENGLISH
dasu	das- dash-	to take out
kasu	kas- kash-	to lend
matsu	mat- mach-	to wait
tatsu	tat- tach-	to stand

  If a verb ends in -*au*, -*iu*, or -*ou*, it is still considered a c-stem verb, and it belongs in this group, even though a vowel remains after the *u* is dropped. The reason is that a missing "*w*" is considered the final consonant of the stem. That *w*, although not used in the affirmative forms, is needed for some of the negative forms. For example:

DICTIONARY FORM	STEM	ENGLISH
shimau	shima(w)-	**to put away**
kau	ka(w)-	**to buy**
iu	i(w)-	**to say**
omou	omo(w)-	**to think**

Some verbs that end in *-eru* and *-iru* belong to the c-stem verb group. Here are a few examples:

DICTIONARY FORM	STEM	ENGLISH
hairu	hair-	**to enter**
kaeru	kaer-	**to return**
shiru	shir-	**to know**
kiru	kir-	**to cut**

Note that *kiru*, **to cut**, is a c-stem verb. When pronounced, the first syllable is stressed. The verb *kiru*, **to wear**, is a v-stem verb (see **§7.3-2**). When pronounced, the second syllable is stressed.

§7.3-2 The Vowel Conjugation

In this group, the verb stems end in a vowel. Therefore, they may be called **v-stem** verbs, as we shall do here. Because the stems are formed by dropping the final **ru**, this is also referred to as the **ru-dropping conjugation**, and the verbs may be called **ru-dropping verbs**.

How can you tell a Vowel Conjugation verb?

Most verbs with dictionary forms which end in *-eru* and *-iru* belong in this group. (For some exceptions, see **§7.3-1**.)

How do you form the stem?

- To form the stem of the verb , drop the final -*ru*.

EXAMPLE

DICTIONARY FORM	STEM	ENGLISH
ageru	age-	to give, to raise
dekiru	deki-	to be able
hajimeru	hajime-	to begin
iru	i-	to be
kangaeru	kangae-	to think
miru	mi-	to see
neru	ne-	to sleep
taberu	tabe-	to eat

§7.4 THE INFINITIVE

The infinitive is also an important base for constructing other verb forms. To form the infinitive, do the following:

- for c-stem verbs, add -*i* to the stem. For example:

DICTIONARY FORM	STEM	INFINITIVE
isogu	isog-	isogi-
kaku	kak-	kaki-
nuru	nur-	nuri-
tobu	tob-	tobi-
shinu	shin-	shini-
yomu	yom-	yomi-

- for v-stem verbs, add *nothing* to the stem. (In this conjugation, the stem and the infinitive are the same.)
  For example:

DICTIONARY FORM	STEM	INFINITIVE
ageru	age-	age-
dekiru	deki-	deki-
hajimeru	hajime-	hajime-
iru	i-	i-
kangaeru	kangae-	kangae-
miru	mi-	mi-

- For the irregular verbs, the forms are as follows:

DICTIONARY FORM	INFINITIVE
kuru	ki-
suru	shi-

§7.5 PLAIN AND POLITE FORMS

The Japanese use different sets, or levels, of verb forms, depending on the politeness requirements of the situation, and the relationship among the speakers. For non-Japanese, using the different politeness levels correctly takes a great deal of experience with the Japanese language and culture.

The two most common levels are called *plain* and *polite*. The plain verb forms are used with immediate family members and close friends and associates. The polite forms have a wider range, and are more appropriate for general use, especially for students of Japanese.

The examples below show two ways of saying the same thing, one plain style, and one polite style. Note the different verb forms.

Plain	Present	da / dictionary form
	Past	**datta** / **-ta, -da**
Polite	Present	desu / -masu
	Past	deshita / -mashita

- Both plain and polite forms are introduced with new verbs throughout this chapter.

EXAMPLES

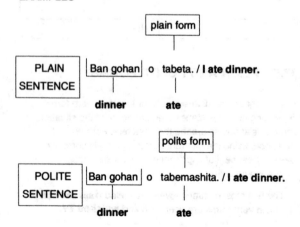

Although readers of this book should use the polite level, both forms must be learned. This is because the plain form can function other than as the main verb. When the main verb of the sentence, the one at the end, is in the polite form, other verbs earlier in the same sentence usually take the plain form.

The examples below show two sentences that say the same thing, one plain style, the other polite. Note that both sentences use a plain verb form, *tabeta*, for **ate**. And keep in mind that the verb at the end determines the politeness level for the entire sentence.

EXAMPLES

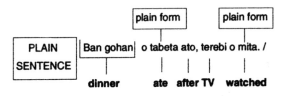

After I ate dinner,
I watched TV.

After I ate dinner,
I watched TV.

In the sections on verbs that follow, both the plain and polite forms will be given. Although there are other, more formal verb forms, these two levels should be appropriate for the reader's needs.

§7.6 THE "TO BE" VERBS

English has one verb to express the meaning **to be**, although that verb takes several forms (**am, is, are, was, were,** etc.). Japanese has three different words, each expressing a particular aspect of the meaning of **to be**: *desu, arimasu,* and *imasu.*

---

desu

Often called the copula, *desu* is used when you want to indicate such things as condition, quality, number, characteristics, or identity. You can understand it more easily if you think of *desu* as meaning not only **is,** but also **equals,** especially with two nouns or noun phrases. If you can substitute **equals** for **is** in an English sentence such as **This equals/is a book** or **Mrs. Smith equals/is my best friend,** *desu* is the word you want.

Although the polite forms *desu* (present) and *deshita* (past) are the ones you will use most often, you should know the following forms as well.

desu / is, equals		Affirmative	Negative
Present	Plain	da	dewa nai
	Polite	desu	dewa arimasen
Past	Plain	datta	dewa nakatta
	Polite	deshita	dewa arimasen deshita
Probable	Plain	darō	dewa nai darō
	Polite	deshō	dewa nai deshō

EXAMPLES

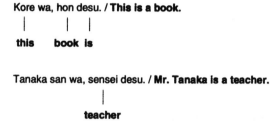

Kore wa, hon desu. / **This is a book.**

   this   book is

Tanaka san wa, sensei desu. / **Mr. Tanaka is a teacher.**

                teacher

Otenki ga, ii desu. / **The weather is good.**

weather good

Otenki ga, warui deshō. / **The weather will probably be bad.**

        bad will probably be

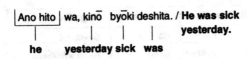

Ano hito | wa, kinō byōki deshita. / **He was sick yesterday.**

| he | yesterday | sick | was |

---

arimasu

Arimasu means **is** or **exists** for the location of inanimate things. It also expresses the idea of English **to have**. If you think of the meaning as **(something) exists/is located (somewhere)**, *arimasu* is the word you want. Because *arimasu* is a stative (non-action) verb, the particle *ni* is used with expressions of location.

EXAMPLE

Hon wa, tēburu no ue ni arimasu. / **The book is on the table.**

| table | 's | top | on |

In the **to have** meaning of *arimasu*, the thing possessed is the subject of the sentence, and takes the particle *ga*.

EXAMPLES

Okane ga arimasu ka. / **Do you have any money?**
(As for you, does money exist?)

| money | is |

Hai, arimasu. / **Yes, I do. (Yes, it exists.)**

| yes |

Here are the other forms of arimasu:

arimasu / is, exists		Affirmative	Negative
Present	Plain	aru	nai
	Polite	arimasu	arimasen
Past	Plain	atta	nakatta
	Polite	arimashita	arimasen deshita
Probable	Plain	aru darō	nai darō
	Polite	aru deshō	nai deshō

EXAMPLES

Fujisan wa, Nihon ni arimasu. / **Mt. Fuji is in Japan.**

         in   is

Ginza ni, sūpā ga arimasu ka. / **Is there a supermarket in Ginza?**

    supermarket

Eki wa, doko ni arimasu ka. / **Where is the station?**

station where

Jisho ga arimasu ka. / **Do you have a dictionary?**

dictionary

Iie, arimasen. / **No, I don't (have a dictionary).**

Koko ni kōen ga arimashita. / **There was a park here.**

here	park	was

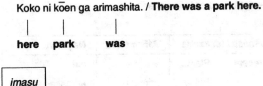

> *imasu*

Imasu is also a stative (non-action) verb used to express **is** or **exists** for location. But *imasu* is used for living things— people, animals, insects (*not* plants). The particle *ni* is used with *imasu* when the location is specified.

Imasu is also used as an auxiliary verb to form the progressive tenses, where it functions just like the English **is**: **He is going, I was going,** etc. Because this meaning of *imasu* is discussed in §7.7-4 and §7.7-5, the examples below will deal with only the locational meaning. First, here are the other forms of *imasu*:

imasu / **is, exists**		**Affirmative**	**Negative**
Present	Plain	iru	inai
	Polite	imasu	imasen
Past	Plain	ita	inakatta
	Polite	imashita	imasen deshita
Probable	Plain	iru darō	inai darō
	Polite	iru deshō	inai deshō

EXAMPLES

Tanaka san wa imasu ka. / **Is Mr. Tanaka here?**

Hai, imasu. / **Yes, he is.**

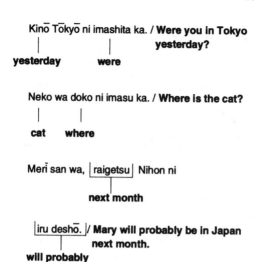

Kinō Tōkyō ni imashita ka. / **Were you in Tokyo yesterday?**

yesterday   were

Neko wa doko ni imasu ka. / **Where is the cat?**

cat   where

Merī san wa, | raigetsu | Nihon ni

next month

| iru deshō. |/ **Mary will probably be in Japan next month.**

will probably be

§7.7 THE INDICATIVE MOOD

The indicative mood allows you to express ordinary, objective statements, questions, etc. Tense refers to the time of the action or state expressed by the verb.

Sometimes Japanese is described as having just two tenses: the past and the non-past. At first, this sounds strange; on second thought, it can be a useful concept. What does it mean? It means that *Japanese does not have a separate future tense.* The past is the past, the non-past is everything else—that is, present and future. Here we will use more conventional terms (present and past), however.

Keep in mind as you look at the different tenses and moods that Japanese verbs do not change their form for gender and number.

§7.7-1 Present Tense

The present tense meanings in Japanese are similar to those of English: incomplete or habitual actions or states. The present tense is used for future time as well; Japanese has no separate future tense.

The plain form of the present tense is the same as the dictionary form, the one from which the stem is derived. The dictionary form was discussed in §7.3, Verb Conjugations.

> plain form, c-stem verbs (see §7.3-1)

iku /   I go, you go, he/she/it goes, we go, they go,

          I will go, you will go, he/she/it will go, we will go, they will go

yomu /   I read, you read, he/she/it reads, we read, they read,

          I will read, you will read, he/she/it will read, we will read, they will read

> plain form, v-stem verbs (see §7.3-1)

miru /   I see, you see, he/she/it sees, we see, they see,

          I will see, you will see, he/she/it will see, we will see, they will see

taberu / I eat, you eat, he/she/it eats, we eat, they eat,

          I will eat, you will eat, he/she/it will eat, we will eat, they will eat

- To form the negative of the plain form, do the following:

> c-stem verbs: add *-anai* to the stem.

| iku / ikanai | **go / don't go** |
| yomu / yomanai | **read / don't read** |

- Note that for c-stem verbs ending in *-au*, *-iu*, or *-ou*, you must add a *w* to the stem before adding *-anai* (see §7.3-1).

shimau / shimawanai	**put away / don't put away**
kau / kawanai	**buy / don't buy**
iu / iwanai	**say / don't say**
omou / omowanai	**think / don't think**

> v-stem verbs: add *-nai* to the stem

hajimeru / hajimenai	**begin / don't begin**
kangaeru / kangaenai	**think / don't think**
taberu / tabenai	**eat / don't eat**
ageru / agenai	**give / don't give**
miru / minai	**see / don't see**

- The polite present is sometimes referred to as the *masu* form. It can be constructed in two different ways.

  Either:

  > Add *-masu* to the infinitive. (See §7.4.)

	isogi + masu	isogimasu / **busy**
	kaki + masu	kakimasu / **write**
c-stem	nuri + masu	nurimasu / **paint**
verbs	tobi + masu	tobimasu / **fly**
	shini + masu	shinimasu / **die**
	yomi + masu	yomimasu / **read**
v-stem	age + masu	agemasu / **give**
verbs	hajime + masu	hajimemasu / **begin**
	kangae + masu	kangaemasu / **think**
	mi + masu	mimasu / **see**
	ki + masu	kimasu / **wear**
	ori + masu	orimasu / **get off**

Or:

> For c-stem verbs, add *-imasu* to the stem.

isogu	isog + imasu	isogimasu / **busy**
kaku	kak + imasu	kakimasu / **write**
nuru	nur + imasu	nurimasu / **paint**

> For v-stem verbs, add *-masu* to the stem.

hajimeru	hajime + masu	hajimemasu / **begin**
kangaeru	kangae + masu	kangaemasu / **think**
miru	mi + masu	mimasu / **see**

To form the polite negative, do the following:

For all verbs, simply change the ending from *masu* to *masen*.

ikimasu / ikimasen	**go / don't go**
wakarimasu / wakarimasen	**understand / don't understand**
kakimasu / kakimasen	**write / don't write**
mimasu / mimasen	**see / don't see**
oshiemasu / oshiemasen	**teach / don't teach**

Here are a few verbs in their present tense conjugations:

Verb		Affirmative	Negative
taberu / **eat**			
Present	Plain	taberu	tabenai
	Polite	tabemasu	tabemasen
nomu / **drink**			
Present	Plain	nomu	nomanai
	Polite	nomimasu	nomimasen
suru / **do**			
Present	Plain	suru	shinai
	Polite	shimasu	shimasen

And some present tense sentences:

EXAMPLES

Watakushi wa, kōhī o | nomimasen. | / **I don't drink coffee.**

           coffee **don't drink**

Tanaka san wa, sushi o mainichi tabemasu. /Mr. Tanaka eats sushi every day.

every day	eat	eats sushi every day.

Ano hitotachi wa, terebi o mimasen. / They don't watch television.

they / television / don't watch / television.

Nihongo ga wakarimasu ka. / Do you understand Japanese?

understand

Kyōto ni ashita ikimasu. / I'll go to Kyoto tomorrow.

tomorrow will go

§7.7-2 Past Tense

Like English, the past tense is used for actions completed in the past (**I ate**, **I studied**, etc.). It is also used to express the equivalent of the English present perfect (**I have walked**, **I have eaten**, etc.).

Forming the plain past tense is easy for v-stem verbs, more complex for c-stem verbs.

For plain form, v-stem verbs: add *-ta* to the stem.

taberu / tabeta	**eat / ate**
oshieru / oshieta	**teach / taught**
miru / mita	**see / saw**
ageru / ageta	**give / gave**

For plain form, c-stem verbs: do the following:

- Look at the *final* syllable in the plain present form (dictionary form) of the verb. Find the syllable in column A below. Change it to the syllable in column B.

	change this→	to this	
omou	u ——→ tta		omotta / **thought**
motsu	tsu ——→ tta		motta / **held**
nuru	ru ——→ tta		nutta / **painted**
nomu	mu ——→ nda		nonda / **drank**
shinu	nu ——→ nda		shinda / **died**
tobu	bu ——→ nda		tonda / **flew**
kiku	ku ——→ ita		kiita / **asked**
oyogu	gu ——→ ida		oyoida / **swam**
hanasu	su ——→ shita		hanashita / **talked**

- To form the negative of the plain past tense, do the following:

c-stem verbs: add -*anakatta* to the stem

iku	itta / ikanakatta	**came / didn't come**
yomu	yonda / yomanakatta	**read / didn't read**
kau(w)	katta / kawanakatta	**bought / didn't buy**
isogu	isoida / isoganakatta	**hurried / didn't hurry**

v-stem verbs: add *-nakatta to the stem.*

hajimeru	hajimeta / hajimenakatta	**began / didn't begin**
taberu	tabeta / tabenakatta	**ate / didn't eat**
ageru	ageta / agenakatta	**gave / didn't give**
miru	mita / minakatta	**saw / didn't see**

For the polite past tense, change the present tense ending from *masu* to *mashita.*

ikimasu / ikimashita	**go / went**
mimasu / mimashita	**see / saw**
kaimasu / kaimashita	**buy / bought**
wakarimasu / wakarimashita	**understand / understood**
tabemasu / tabemashita	**eat / ate**
shimasu / shimashita	**do / did**
kimasu / kimashita	**come / came**

For the negative of the polite past, add the word *deshita* to the polite present negative.

tabemasen / tabemasen deshita	**don't eat / didn't eat**
ikimasen / ikimasen deshita	**don't go / didn't go**
hashirimasen / hashirimasen deshita	**don't run / didn't run**
kaimasen / kaimasen deshita	**don't buy / didn't buy**

Here are a few verbs in their past tense conjugations:

Verb		Affirmative	Negative
kiru / **to put on (clothes)**			
Past	Plain	kita	kinakatta
	Polite	kimashita	kimasen deshita
yomu / **to read**			
Past	Plain	yonda	yomanakatta
	Polite	yomimashita	yomimasen deshita
suru / **to do**			
Past	Plain	shita	shinakatta
	Polite	shimashita	shimasen deshita

And some past tense sentences:

EXAMPLES

Itsu kimashita ka. / **When did you come?**

when came

Mada | shimasen deshita. | / **I haven't done it yet.**

   | |

yet   **haven't done**

Owarimashita. / **It's finished.**

    |

 finished

Doko de kaimashita ka. / **Where did you buy it?**

         |

       bought

Naze | ikimasen deshita | ka. / **Why didn't you go?**

  | |

why   **didn't go**

§7.7-3 The Gerund

Often referred to as the "-te form," the gerund is a useful form of the Japanese verb. Alone, it does not have tense or mood. But it combines with other verb forms to create tenses and moods, such as the continuous tenses and the imperative mood, for example. It has other uses as well.

One caution: The term "gerund" may be misleading. In English, a gerund is the -ing form of a verb when functioning as a noun (**I like swimming**, **Reading is my favorite hobby**, etc.). The Japanese gerund is a verb form, not a noun. Indeed, in the progressive tenses, it functions much like the English **-ing** form.

Gerunds are regular in form and easy to construct.

Start with the plain past tense (see §7.7-2), and change the final -*a* to -*e*.

Present	Past	Gerund
aruku / **walk**	aruita	aruite
kiku / **ask, listen**	kiita	kiite
taberu / **eat**	tabeta	tabete
hanasu / **speak**	hanashita	hanashite
yomu / **read**	yonda	yonde

One important use of the gerund is when listing actions in a neutral sequence (with no strong contrast or emphasis) within a sentence. All but the last verb are gerunds.

EXAMPLE

Sūpā ni itte, niku o katte, uchi ni

 | | | | | | |

 went meat bought

kaerimashita. / **I went to the supermarket, bought**

 | **some meat, and returned home.**

 returned

§7.7-4 Present Progressive

Japanese uses the present progressive for action in progress or continuous action, state of being, and also to express the meaning of the English present perfect.

Unlike English, it cannot be used to express future meaning (**Tomorrow he's going to New York**, or **I'm getting my degree next year**, etc.).

To form the present progressive, start with the gerund, and add the appropriate form of the verb *iru*. The plain form is used in informal conversation, of course. The polite form, appropriate for general use, is given here. Note that *iru* when used alone as a verb can only refer to living things. With the gerund, it is used for inanimate things as well.

Affirmative	Negative
aruite imasu / **walking**	aruite imasen / **not walking**
kiite imasu / **listening**	kiite imasen / **not listening**
tabete imasu / **eating**	tabete imasen / **not eating**
hanashite imasu / **speaking**	hanashite imasen / **not speaking**
yonde imasu / **reading**	yonde imasen / **not reading**
nonde imasu / **drinking**	nonde imasen / **not drinking**

Affirmative	Negative
motte imasu / **holding**	motte imasen / **not holding**
oyoide imasu / **swimming**	oyoide imasen / **not swimming**

When the meaning of this tense is an action in progress, the verb is often transitive (a verb that takes an object). This is similar to the English present progressive.

EXAMPLES

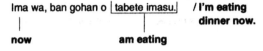

Ima wa, ban gohan o tabete imasu. / **I'm eating dinner now.**

now   am eating

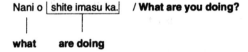

Nani o shite imasu ka. / **What are you doing?**

what   are doing

Eigo o benkyō shite imasu. / **I'm studying English.**

am studying

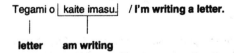

Tegami o kaite imasu. / **I'm writing a letter.**

letter   am writing

When the meaning is a state of being, the verb is often intransitive (a verb that doesn't take an object). This is not like an English progressive tense usage; the explanations after the examples below should help clarify the meanings.

EXAMPLES

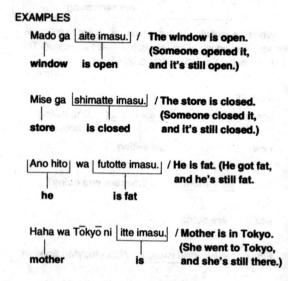

Mado ga | aite imasu. | / **The window is open.**
| |
window   is open   **(Someone opened it, and it's still open.)**

Mise ga | shimatte imasu. | / **The store is closed.**
| |
store   is closed   **(Someone closed it, and it's still closed.)**

| Ano hito | wa | futotte imasu. | / **He is fat. (He got fat, and he's still fat.**
| |
he   is fat

Haha wa Tōkyō ni | itte imasu. | / **Mother is in Tokyo.**
| |
mother   is   **(She went to Tokyo, and she's still there.)**

Tsukarete imasu. / **I'm tired. (I got tired, and**
| **I'm still tired.)**
tired

The present progressive can express the English present perfect tense—an action that began in the past and continues through the present. In the following sentences, notice how the time element, **for five years**, results in a present perfect meaning. Without it, the meaning is simply continuous action.

EXAMPLES

Kyōto ni gonen kan | sunde imasu. | / **I have been**
     | | **living in Kyoto**
  five years for   **am living**   **for five years.**

Kyōto ni sunde imasu. / **I'm living in Kyoto.**

§7.7-5 Past Progressive

The past progressive is used for past continuous action or
state of being.

The form is easy: start with the gerund, and change
imasu to the past form: *imashita*. The negative is the gerund
plus the negative past of *imashita*, which is *imasen deshita*.

Affirmative	Negative
aruite imashita / **was walking**	aruite imasen deshita / **wasn't walking**
kiite imashita / **was listening**	kiite imasen deshita / **wasn't listening**
tabete imashita / **was eating**	tabete imasen deshita / **wasn't eating**
hanashite imashita / **was speaking** /	hanashite imasen deshita / **wasn't speaking**
yonde imashita / **was reading**	yonde imasen deshita / **wasn't reading**
nonde imashita / **was drinking**	nonde imasen deshita / **wasn't drinking**

Affirmative	Negative
motte imashita / **was holding**	motte imasen deshita / **wasn't holding**
oyoide imashita / **was swimming**	oyoide imasen deshita / **wasn't swimming**

Here are some examples of past continuous action.

EXAMPLES

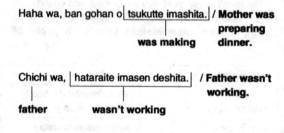

Haha wa, ban gohan o | tsukutte imashita. | / **Mother was preparing dinner.**
                  was making

Chichi wa, | hataraite imasen deshita. | / **Father wasn't working.**
father   **wasn't working**

Kyonen Nihongo o | benkyō shite imashita. | / **Last year I was studying Japanese.**
last year   **was studying**

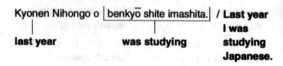

Neko ga, | isu no | ue de | nete imashita. | / **The cat was sleeping on the chair.**
cat   **chair's top**   **was sleeping**

The following examples show past states of being.

EXAMPLES

Denki ga | tsuite imashita. | / **The light was on.**

light   was on

Doa ga | aite imashita. | / **The door was open.**

door   was open

Ano hito wa | yasete imashita. | / **She was thin.**

was thin

Tsukarete imasen deshita. / **I wasn't tired.**

tired

§7.8 THE PRESUMPTIVE MOOD

Sometimes called the "probable" mood, this has no exact
equivalent in English, although it is important in Japanese.
It enables speakers to use a verb form that can express
probability, *belief*, or *intention* without being too direct. This
mood has two sets of forms, one indicating probability, the
second indicating intention.

$$\boxed{\text{da}\overline{\text{ro}},\ \text{desh}\overline{\text{o}} \text{ form}}$$

This form expresses the speaker's belief that something will probably happen. It is easily constructed by adding *darō* or *deshō* (plain and polite, respectively) to the plain, or dictionary form, of the verb. This works for the negative of the plain form as well, and also for the past forms.

Present	
Plain	**Polite**
kuru darō	kuru deshō / **will probably come**
iku darō	iku deshō / **will probably go**
taberu darō	taberu deshō / **will probably eat**
Negative	
konai darō	konai deshō / **will probably not come**
ikanai darō	ikanai deshō / **will probably not go**
tabenai darō	tabenai deshō / **will probably not eat**
Past	
kita darō	kita deshō / **probably came**
itta darō	itta deshō / **probably went**
tabeta darō	tabeta deshō / **probably ate**
Negative	
konakatta darō	konakatta deshō / **probably didn't come**
ikanakatta darō	ikanakatta deshō / **probably didn't go**
tabanakatta darō	tabenakatta deshō / **probably didn't eat**

The examples below show some expanded dimensions of these forms, which can also be translated as **suppose, wonder, guess,** etc.

EXAMPLES

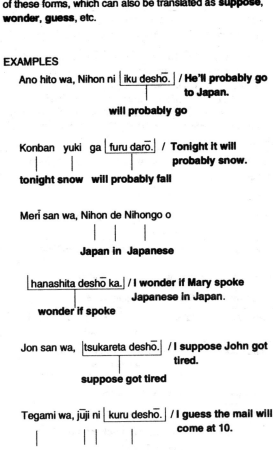

Ano hito wa, Nihon ni ⌐iku deshō.⌐ / **He'll probably go to Japan.**

will probably go

Konban yuki ga ⌐furu darō.⌐ / **Tonight it will probably snow.**

tonight snow will probably fall

Merī san wa, Nihon de Nihongo o

Japan in Japanese

⌐hanashita deshō ka.⌐ / **I wonder if Mary spoke Japanese in Japan.**

wonder if spoke

Jon san wa, ⌐tsukareta deshō.⌐ / **I suppose John got tired.**

suppose got tired

Tegami wa, jūji ni ⌐kuru deshō.⌐ / **I guess the mail will come at 10.**

mail 10 at guess will come

$-\bar{o}$, $-y\bar{o}$ / $-mash\bar{o}$ forms

These differ somewhat in the plain and polite forms.

First consider the plain form, $-\bar{o}$, $-y\bar{o}$. As a final verb at the end of a sentence, it expresses the speaker's intention. Considered abrupt, it is used mostly by men. It can also mean "Let's (do something)," but for this, the *-mashō* form is preferred. As a medial verb (not at the end of the sentence), it expresses intention or probability. The forms are made as follows:

- For c-stem verbs, start with the plain, or dictionary form, and change the final *-u* to *-ō*

Present	Presumptive
nuru / **paint**	nurō / **will probably paint, will/ let's paint**
kiku / **ask**	kikō / **will probably ask, will/let's ask**

- For v-stem verbs, start with the stem, and add *-yō*.

Present	Stem	Presumptive
taberu / **eat**	tabe-	tabeyō / **will probably eat, will/let's eat**
miru / **see**	mi-	miyō / **will probably see, will/let's see**

- The irregular verb forms are as follows:

suru / **do**	shiyō / **will probably do, will/let's do**
kuru / **come**	koyō / **will probably come, will/let's come**

- The negative forms, infrequently used, are not needed here.

Note how the ō and yō forms are used in medial and final position, and the differences in meaning.

EXAMPLES

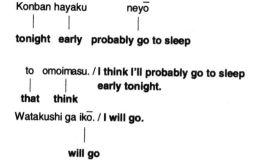

Konban hayaku   neyō

tonight early probably go to sleep

to omoimasu. / I think I'll probably go to sleep

that think   early tonight.

Watakushi ga ikō. / I will go.

will go

Tabeyō. / Let's eat.

Now look at the polite form, -mashō. This can express several things: the speaker's intention to do something, a polite description of the probability of someone else's doing something, or, most common, the idea of "Let's," or "Shall we?"

To construct this form, add -mashō to the infinitive of the verb.

Plain	Infinitive	-mashō Form
yomu / **read**	yomi-	yomimashō / **let's read**
miru / **see**	mi-	mimashō / **let's see**
taberu / **eat**	tabe-	tabemashō / **let's eat**
iku / **go**	iki-	ikimashō / **let's go**

Here are some examples of some common uses of this form:

EXAMPLES

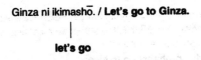

Ginza ni ikimashō. / **Let's go to Ginza.**

let's go

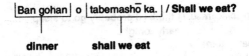

Ban gohan | o | tabemashō ka. | / **Shall we eat?**

dinner   shall we eat

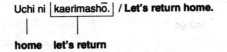

Uchi ni | kaerimashō. | / **Let's return home.**

home   let's return

Watakushi ga shimashō. / **I'll do it.**

will do

Jon san ga kimashō. / **John will probably come.**

will probably come

- Note that the last sentence above would mean the same thing using the *deshō* form. For example:

Jon san ga | kuru deshō. | / **John will probably come.**

will probably come.

§7.9 THE IMPERATIVE MOOD

The true *imperative*, or *command*, form in Japanese is said
by a superior to an inferior. It is too abrupt for most usage.
However, you should recognize it.

The imperative is formed by adding *-e* to the stem of
c-stem verbs, and *-ro* to the stem of v-stem verbs. To form
the negative imperatives, add *-na* to the plain present form
of the verb.

Plain	Imperative	Imperative (Negative)
iku / **go**	ike / **go!**	ikuna / **don't go!**
kiku / **listen**	kike / **listen!**	kikuna / **don't listen!**
taberu / **eat**	tabero / **eat!**	taberuna / **don't eat!**
miru / **look**	miro / **look!**	miruna / **don't look!**

A somewhat less harsh form is made by adding *-nasai* to
the infinitive form of the verb. This is not used with negative
forms.

iku / **go**	ikinasai / **go**
taberu / **eat**	tabenasai / **eat**

EXAMPLES

Yukkuri hanashinasai. / **Speak slowly.**

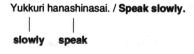

slowly   speak

Koko ni kinasai. / **Come here.**

here   come

The form of the imperative commonly used for polite requests or commands is the gerund, or *-te* form, with the word *kudasai*.

kuru / **come**	Kite kudasai. / **Please come.**
taberu / **eat**	Tabete kudasai. / **Please eat.**
suwaru / **sit down**	Suwatte kudasai. / **Please sit down.**
kiku / **listen**	Kiite kudasai. / **Please listen.**
hanasu / **speak**	Hanashite kudasai. / **Please speak.**

EXAMPLES

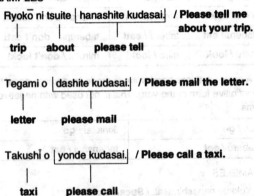

Ryokō ni tsuite | hanashite kudasai. / **Please tell me about your trip.**
trip   about   please tell

Tegami o | dashite kudasai. / **Please mail the letter.**
letter   please mail

Takushī o | yonde kudasai. / **Please call a taxi.**
taxi   please call

For the negative of this structure, add *-de kudasai* to the negative of the plain present form.

Ikanaide kudasai. / **Please don't go.**
Shinpai shinaide kusasai. / **Please don't worry.**

Kudasai can also be used when requesting an object. In this usage another verb form is not needed.

EXAMPLES

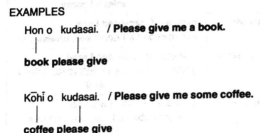

Hon o kudasai. / **Please give me a book.**

book please give

Kōhi o kudasai. / **Please give me some coffee.**

coffee please give

§7.10 THE CONDITIONAL MOOD

In Japanese, there are several ways of conveying the conditional, or "if" meaning. Although they can, in many cases, be used interchangeably, there are slight differences in meaning.

-eba form

This is sometimes called the "provisional" form, because it means "if" in the sense of "provided something happens (now or in the future)." In the negative form, it can mean "unless."

For the *-eba* form, drop the final *-u* of the dictionary form of the verb and add *-eba*. For the negative, drop the final *-i* of the plain negative form and add *-kereba*.

Plain	Conditional
kuru / **come**	kureba / **if, provided I (you, etc.) come** konakereba / **if I don't come,** **unless I come**
miru / **see**	mireba / **if, provided I see** minakereba / **if I don't see, unless I see**
yomu / **read**	yomeba / **if, provided I read** yomanakereba / **if I don't read, unless** **I read**
taberu / **eat**	tabereba / **if, provided I eat** tabenakereba / **if I don't eat, unless** **I eat**

EXAMPLES

Isshōkenmei | benkyō sureba, | Nihongo o

hard   if study   Japanese

oboemasu. / **If you study hard, you'll learn**
                Japanese.

will learn

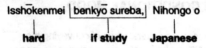

| Ano hito | ni aereba | shiwase desu. | / **If I meet him, I'll**
                                    be happy.

him   if meet   will be happy

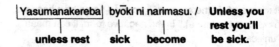

| Yasumanakereba | byōki ni narimasu. / **Unless you**
                                  rest you'll

unless rest   sick   become   **be sick.**

With verbal adjectives (-*i* adjectives), drop the -*i* and add *kereba*. For the negative, use the adverbial form (yasuku) [see §8.2-3] and add *nakereba*. For example:

Adjective	Conditional
yasui / **cheap**	yasukereba / **if it's cheap, if it were cheap** yasukunakereba / **if it's not cheap, unless it's cheap**

EXAMPLES

Yasukereba, kaimasu. / **If it's cheap, I'll buy it.**

if cheap **buy**

Samukereba, obā o kimasu. / **If it's cold, I'll put on an overcoat.**

if cold **coat** **put on**

Omoshirokereba, yomimasu. / **If it's interesting, I'll read it.**

if interesting **read**

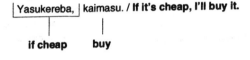

-*tara* form

The -*tara* form can express a wide range of conditional "when" and "if" meaning: past occurrence, hypothetical conditions in the past, future or habitual action. (See the forms below.)

To construct the -*tara* form, start with the plain past verb form and add -*ra*.

tabetara /   **if I (you, etc.) should eat (it)**

                   if I (you, etc.) were to eat (it)

                   when I (you, etc.) eat (it)

                   when I (you, etc.) ate (it)

For the negative, do the same: tabenakattara / **If I (you, etc.) didn't eat (it).**

EXAMPLES

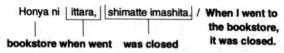

Honya ni | ittara, | shimatte imashita. | / **When I went to the bookstore, it was closed.**

bookstore   when went   was closed

Benkyō shitara, | wakatta deshō. | / **If I had studied, I would have understood.**

if had studied   understood

Kōhī o nondara, | neraremasen. | / **When I drink coffee, I can't sleep.**

coffee when drink   can't sleep

Notice the use of -*tara* forms with -*i* and -*na* adjectives and with nouns.

EXAMPLES

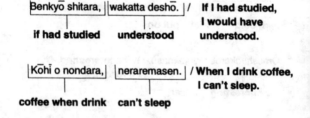

Takakattara | kaimasen. | / **If it's expensive, I won't buy it.**

if expensive   won't buy

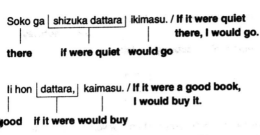

Soko ga | shizuka dattara | ikimasu. / **If it were quiet**
| | | **there, I would go.**

there | **if were quiet** | **would go**

Ii hon | dattara, | kaimasu. / **If it were a good book,**
| | | **I would buy it.**

good | **if it were** | **would buy**

Other useful conditional forms are *nara* and *to*.

nara

with verbs:	Present: iku nara / **if I (you, etc.) go** Past: itta nara / **if I had gone**
with verbal adjectives	Present: ōkii nara / **if it is / were big** Past: ōkikatta nara / **if it had been big**
with adjectival nouns	Present: kirei nara / **if it is / were pretty** Past: kirei datta nara / **if it had been pretty**
with nouns	gakusei nara / **if I am / were a student**

Similar to the *-tara* forms in meaning, *nara* can be used for if and **after**. In some uses, it has a strong contrary-to-fact element, like the subjunctive mood of English.

EXAMPLES

Watakushi ga kanemochi nara   yotto o
| | |
rich person **if** **sailboat**

| kaimasu. | / **If I were rich, I would buy a sailboat.**
|
would buy

Isogu nara, chikatetsu de ikinasai. / **If you're in a hurry,**
  | | | | **take a subway.**

hurry if   subway   take

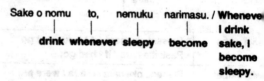

to

to is used with the present forms of verbs and verbal
adjectives, adjectival nouns, and with nouns. In many cases
the meaning is the same as that of the *-tara* or *-eba* forms.

EXAMPLES

Sake o nomu to,   nemuku narimasu. / **Whenever**
    | | | | **I drink**

       drink whenever sleepy become   **sake, I**
                                     become
                                     sleepy.

Tenki ga ii   to,   kōen ni ikimasu. / **When/if**
    | | | | | **the weather**

weather good when/if park   go   **is good, I**
                                       will go to
                                       the park.

§7.11 THE POTENTIAL MOOD

To express the idea of capability or possibility (**can** or **be
able to** in English), add *-eru* (plain) or *-emasu* (polite) to the
stem of c-stem verbs, and *-rareru* (plain) or *-raremasu*
(polite) to the stem of v-stem verbs. The negatives are
formed regularly: add *-enai* / *-emasen* to the stem of c-stem
verbs, and *-rarenai* / *-raremasen* to the stem of v-stem verbs.

EXAMPLES

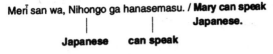

Merī san wa, Nihongo ga hanasemasu. / **Mary can speak Japanese.**

Japanese — can speak

Nanji ni aemasu ka. / **What time can I see you?**

what time — can see

Kyō ikenai nara, ashita ikemasu ka. / **If you can't go today, can you go tomorrow?**

today — can't go — if — tomorrow — can go — ?

Another way to express the potential is as follows:

Place the appropriate form of the verb *dekiru* / **can do** after a noun (plus the particle *ga*).

EXAMPLES

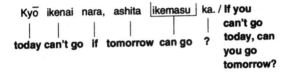

Nihongo ga dekimasu. / **I can speak Japanese.**

Japanese — can do

Tenisu ga dekimasu. / **I can play tennis.**

tennis — can do

Ryōri ga dekimasen. / **I can't cook.**

cooking   can't do

A verb form can be used with this structure as well, but it must first be nominalized, or made into a noun form. To nominalize a verb, do the following:

- Add the word *koto* to the plain, or dictionary form, of the verb. Then it can be used with *ga* and *dekiru* / *dekimasu.*

  EXAMPLES

  Nihongo o yomu koto ga dekimasu. / **I can read Japanese.**

  Japanese read   can do

  Meri san wa, oyogu koto ga dekimasen. / **Mary can't swim.**

  swim   can't do

  Kinō, Tanaka san ni au koto ga

  yesterday   see

  dekimashita. / **Yesterday, I could see Ms. Tanaka.**

  could do

§7.12 THE PASSIVE VOICE

Japanese has two ways of using the passive. The first is with transitive verbs, as in English. In such sentences, the "doer" may or may not be expressed. (**My wallet was stolen,** *or* **My wallet was stolen by a pickpocket.**)

To form the passive, add *-areru*, *-aremasu* to the stems of c-stem verbs, and *-rareru*, *-raremasu* to the stems of v-stem verbs. For the negative, add *-arenai*, *-aremasen* to the stems of c-stem verbs, and *-rarenai*, *-raremasen* to the stems of v-stem verbs.

---

nusumu / **steal**, nusumareru, nusumaremasu / **is stolen**
oikakeru / **chase**, oikakerareru, oikakeraremasu /
is chased

EXAMPLES

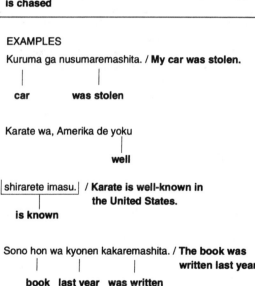

Kuruma ga nusumaremashita. / **My car was stolen.**
    car   was stolen

Karate wa, Amerika de yoku
                     well

shirarete imasu. / **Karate is well-known in**
    is known   **the United States.**

Sono hon wa kyonen kakaremashita. / **The book was**
                         written last year.
  book last year was written

Neko wa, inu ni oikakeraremashita. / **The cat was**
                     chased by a dog.
  cat   dog by was chased

So | mirarete imasu. | / It is seen that way.

that way   it is seen

- Note that the use of this type of passive is more limited in Japanese than in English. While passive forms are grammatically possible for many verbs, the resulting sentences may be awkward.

The second way of using the passive in Japanese, for which English has no corresponding use, may be called the "adversity" passive. You can think of it as the "too bad" or "regrettably" passive. This means that something happened to someone and it had an adverse effect on that person. The verb may be transitive or intransitive. Because this is quite unlike English, read the following sentences carefully, especially the translations.

- Note the use of *ni* in the passive sentences below.

EXAMPLES

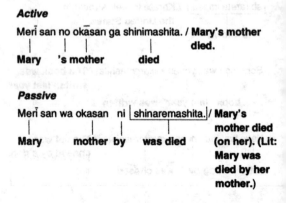

Active

Merī san no okāsan ga shinimashita. / Mary's mother died.

Mary   's mother   died

Passive

Merī san wa okāsan ni | shinaremashita. |/ Mary's mother died (on her). (Lit: Mary was died by her mother.)

Mary   mother   by   was died

Active

Ame ga furimashita. / **It rained. (The rain fell.)**

| |
rain   fell

Passive

Tanaka san wa ame ni furaremashita. / **Mr. Tanaka**
               | | | **was caught in**
         rain by was fallen **the rain. (Lit:**
                         Mr. Tanaka was
                         fallen by rain.)

§7.13 THE CAUSATIVE

The causative forms in Japanese express the idea of
making or causing someone to do something: **I made my
brother clean his room.** It also can mean **let** or **allow**:
Please let me go.

To form the causative, add *-aseru, -asemasu* to the stem of
c-stem verbs (*-asenai, -asemasen* for the negative), and add
-saseru, -sasemasu to the stem of v-stem verbs (*-sasenai,
-sasemasen* for the negative).

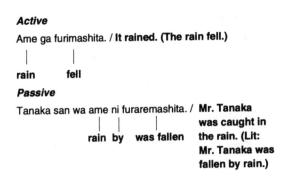

yomu / **read**, yomaseru, yomasemasu / **make (someone)
                                  read
                                  let (someone)
                                  read**
taberu / **eat**, tabesaseru, tabesasemasu / **make
                                (someone) eat
                                let (someone)
                                eat**

EXAMPLES

Merī san o mise ni ikasemashita. / I made Mary go to the store.

store to made go

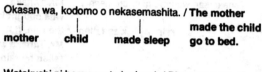

Okāsan wa, kodomo o nekasemashita. / The mother made the child go to bed.

mother child made sleep

Watakushi ni harawasete kudasai. / Please let me pay.

let pay please

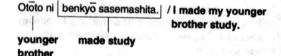

Otōto ni | benkyō sasemashita. | / I made my younger brother study.

younger
brother made study

§7.14 THE CAUSATIVE PASSIVE

The causative passive form expresses the idea that the subject of the sentence is made to do something in the sense of being forced.

- To form the causative passive, add *-aserareru*, *-aseraremasu* to the stem of c-stem verbs (*-aserarenai*, *-aseraremasen* for the negative), and add *-saserareru*, *-saseraremasu* to the stem of v-stem verbs (*-saserarenai*, *-saseraremasen* for the negative).

iku / **go**	ikaserareru, ikaseraremasu / **be made to go**
taberu / **eat**	tabesaserareru, tabesaseraremasu / **be made to eat**

EXAMPLES

Kyōkasho o | kawaseraremashita. | / **I was made to buy a textbook.**

textbook   was made to buy

Kodomo wa, miruku o nomaseraremashita. / **The child was made to drink (his) milk.**

child   milk   was made to drink

Jon san wa, | asa gohan | o

breakfast

| tsukuraseraremashita. | / **John was forced to make breakfast.**

was forced to make

§7.15 THE GIVING AND RECEIVING VERBS

Japanese has several verbs for conveying the meaning of
giving and *receiving*. Choosing which one to use involves
the relative status of the giver and receiver. It also involves
the direction of the action, in the sense of giving *to* and
receiving *from*.

- The following verbs are used to describe someone's giving
something to you, the speaker, or to someone in your
in-group, as in the diagram below the box.

> To say **to give kindly** (to me or my in-group: family,
> **friends, etc.**), use:
> *kureru*
> *kudasaru* (use for referring to superiors)

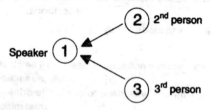

EXAMPLES

Haha ga watakushi ni kuremashita. / **My mother gave it**
   | | | | **to me.**
my mother me   to   gave

Kore wa tomodachi ga kureta hon desu. / **This is the**
 | | | | | **book my**
this   friend   gave book is   **friend gave**
                                       me.

Sensei ga jisho o kudasaimashita. / **The teacher gave**
   | | | **me a dictionary.**
teacher dictionary   gave

- The following verbs are used for **I give, he gives**, etc., as in
the diagram below the box.

To say **give**, use:

ageru

sashiageru (use for speaking to or referring to superiors)

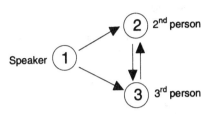

EXAMPLES

Chichi ni ocha o agemashita. / **I gave my father some tea.**

father	**tea**	**gave**

Meri san wa, Jon san ni chizu o agemashita. / **Mary gave John a map.**

map	**gave**

Tanaka san wa, shachō ni hana o

company president **flowers**

sashiagemashita. / **Mrs. Tanaka gave flowers to the company president.**

gave

- The following verbs are used for **receive**, as in the diagram below the box.

> To say **to receive**, use:
> *morau*
> *itadaku* (use for speaking to or referring to superiors)

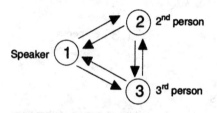

Speaker ①
② 2nd person → 2nd person
③ 3rd person

EXAMPLES

Jon san wa, tomodachi ni rekōdo
     friend from record

 o moraimashita. / **John received a record from his friend.**
 received

Chichi wa, kaisha kara bōnasu o
father company from bonus

 moraimashita. / **Father received a bonus from the company.**
 received

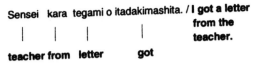

Sensei kara tegami o itadakimashita. / I got a letter
from the
teacher.

teacher from letter got

The giving and receiving verbs are often used as
auxiliaries after the gerund, or -te form of another verb. In
this usage, the relationship between the giver and the
receiver is as described in the verbs given above. When
speaking to or about a superior, be sure to use the
appropriate verb.

Keep in mind that these forms can mean not just giving or
receiving something tangible, but also giving or receiving the
action or sense of the verb.

tsukuru / make   tsukutte kureru, tsukutte kudasaru

EXAMPLES

Haha ga, watakushi ni ban gohan o

mother   dinner

tsukutte kuremashita. / Mother made dinner for me.

(kindly) made

Merī san no okāsan ga, watakushi ni sētā o

Mary 's mother   me   sweater

ande kudasaimashita. / Mary's mother knitted me
a sweater.

(kindly) knitted

> *kau* / **buy**   *katte ageru, katte sashiageru*

EXAMPLES

Tanaka san ga, Jon san ni sore o
|
it

| katte agemashita. | / **Mr. Tanaka bought it for John.**

bought

Suzuki san wa, shachō ni nekutai o
company necktie
president

| katte sashiagemashita. | / **Mr. Suzuki bought the**
company president a tie.

bought

> *iku* / **go**   *itte morau, itte itadaku*

EXAMPLES

Ane ni kaimono ni | itte moraimashita. | / **I had my elder**
elder shopping   **sister go**
sister   **had go**   **shopping**
                                            for me.

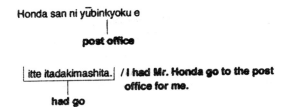

Honda san ni yūbinkyoku e
|
post office

itte itadakimashita. / **I had Mr. Honda go to the post office for me.**
|
had go

§7.16 HONORIFIC AND HUMBLE FORMS

Using the correct language to reflect relationships is important to the Japanese. This means expressing the appropriate degree of respect or deference to the listener, and the appropriate degree of humility about oneself or one's family. The speaker's attitude toward the listener or the person being spoken about is the key. Honorific language elevates someone else; humble language lowers oneself.

Using the honorific and humble verb forms confidently takes a good deal of experience with Japanese culture, but the forms themselves are not difficult to learn.

The honorifics of verbs take several forms.

One honorific form is the passive form itself (see §7.12).

Plain Form	Passive and Honorific Form
aruku / **walk**	arukareru
kaeru / **change**	kaerareru
suru / **do**	sareru
kuru / **come**	korareru

Another set of honorific forms can be made as follows:

> *o* + infinitive + *desu*

> *yobu* / **call**   *oyobi desu (honorific form)*

EXAMPLES

Shachō ga | oyobi desu. | / **The company president is**
         | | **calling you.**
company   is calling
president

Shachō ga oyobi deshita. / **The company president**
                          was calling you.

> *o* + infinitive + *ni naru*

EXAMPLES

Shachō ga | oyobi ni narimashita. | / **The company**
                                       president called
                  called   **you.**

Hon o | oyomi ni narimashita | ka. / **Have you read this**
                                      book?
book   read

> *o* + infinitive + *kudasai* / **Please (do it).**

EXAMPLES

Tanaka san o | oyobi kudasai. | / **Please call Mr. Tanaka.**

                  please call

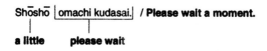

Shōshō │ omachi kudasai. │ / **Please wait a moment.**

a little   **please wait**

The humble forms can be constructed as follows:

> o + infinitive + *suru*

EXAMPLES

Watakushi ga Tanaka san o│oyobi shimasu.│/ I'll call Mr.
                                            Tanaka.

will call

Hiru made ni │ onaoshi shimasu. │ / I'll fix it by noon.

noon by   **will fix**

> o + infinitive + *itasu*

EXAMPLES

Sugu │ omochi itashimasu. │ / I'll bring it immediately.

immediately   will bring

Kasa o │okashi itashimashō ka.│ / Shall I lend you an
                                   umbrella?

umbrella   **shall lend**

Some verbs have special honorific and humble forms.
Following are a few commonly used examples.

Verb	Honorific	Humble
iku / **go**	irassharu	mairu
kuru / **come**	irassharu	mairu
iru / **be**	irassharu	oru
suru / **do**	nasaru	itasu
iu / **say**	ossharu	mōsu
taberu / **eat**	meshiagaru	itadaku
miru / **see**	goran ni naru	haiken suru

§7.17 CLAUSES

> **Dependent Clauses**

Unlike English, independent clauses in Japanese cannot be strung together in one sentence and joined by a conjunction like "and." In Japanese, the main or independent clause comes at the *end* of the sentence, and other clauses are *dependent*. Following are some basic ways in which dependent clauses are linked to the main, or independent clause.

> **. . . -te . . . -te**

- The *-te*, or gerund form of the verb can be used to indicate sequential, parallel, or causal relationships of dependent clauses. Look at each in turn.

| Sequential: | As the name implies, this form is used for actions that occur in a time sequence: first, then, then, etc. |

EXAMPLE

Ginza e itte kaimono o shite, uchi e
   | | | |
went shopping did home

kaerimashita. / **I went to Ginza, did some shopping, and returned home.**
   |
returned

| Parallel: | The action here is parallel, or can take place at the same time. |

EXAMPLES

Yamada san wa Ginza e itte, watakushi wa Shinjuku e
                    |
                   went

ikimashita. / **Ms. Yamada went to Ginza, and I went to Shinjuku.**
  |
went

Kono heya wa, hirokute akarukute
 | | | |
this room   is spacious is bright

rippa desu. / **This room is spacious and bright and gorgeous.**
  |
is gorgeous

| Causal: | The dependent clause shows the cause, the main clause shows the effect. The cause-effect relationship need not be a strong one, however, for the -*te* form to be used. |

EXAMPLES

Sensō ga owatte ureshii desu. / **I'm glad because the war is over.**

| | | | |
| war | is over | glad | am |

Yamada san wa, byōki de kimasen. / **Ms. Yamada isn't coming because she's sick.**

| | | |
| sick | is | isn't coming |

Kono heya wa akarukute kimochi ga ii desu. / **I feel good because this room is bright.**

| | | |
| this room | is bright | feeling is good |

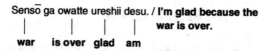

. . . -*tari* . . . -*tari*

- This form is used for **do things like . . .** or **sometimes this, sometimes that.**

EXAMPLES

Shūmatsu wa, nani o shimasu ka. / **What do you do on**
   | | | **weekends?**
weekends what   do

Eiga o mitari, tenisu o shitari shimasu. / **I do things like**
  | | | | | **seeing a movie**
movie like tennis   like   do   and/or playing
  seeing   playing   tennis.

Haha no ryōri wa, oishikattari mazukattari
  | | | | |
mother's cooking sometimes sometimes
                     good   bad

shimasu. / **My mother's cooking is sometimes**
  | **good, sometimes bad.**
does

> ... -shi ... -shi

This form is used for **and in addition, and what's more.**

EXAMPLES

Kono shūmatsu wa iroiro shimashita. / **I did various**
  | | | | **things this**
this weekend   various did   weekend.
               things

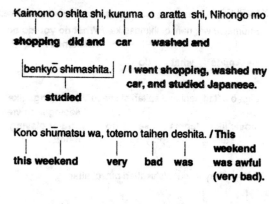

Kaimono o shita shi, kuruma o aratta shi, Nihongo mo
shopping did and car washed and

benkyō shimashita. / I went shopping, washed my
car, and studied Japanese.
studied

Kono shūmatsu wa, totemo taihen deshita. / This
this weekend very bad was weekend
was awful
(very bad).

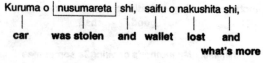

Kuruma o nusumareta shi, saifu o nakushita shi,
car was stolen and wallet lost and
what's more

inu ni kamaremashita. / My car was stolen, I
dog by was bitten lost my wallet, and
what's more, I was
bitten by a dog.

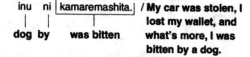

Relative Clauses

Japanese does not have relative pronouns like the English
who, that, which, for use in relative clauses such as **The
man who arrived is my friend.** Instead, the relative clause,
ending with the plain form of the verb, comes *before* the
word it modifies.

EXAMPLES

Watakushi $\frac{ga/}{no}$ itsumo iku restoran wa, Ginza

| | | | |
| I | always | go | restaurant |

ni arimasu. / **The restaurant that I always go to is**
| | **in Ginza.**
in is

Kondo no ryokō de itta tokoro wa, Amerika to

| | | |
this trip went places
time

Kanada deshita. / **The places that I went to on this**
| | **trip were America and Canada.**
Canada were

§7.18 COMMON EXPRESSIONS WITH VERBS AND ADJECTIVES

The following forms are useful, some with verbs, some with both verbs and adjectives. If you use the *-de*, *demo*, or *dewa* forms, they can be used with nouns or adjectival nouns as well.

> *-temo ii desu* / **It's okay if . . .**
> **You may . . .**

EXAMPLES

Takakutemo ii desu. / **It's okay (even) if it's expensive.**
| | |
if expensive okay is

Tabetemo   ii   desu. / You may eat.
   | | |

if eat   okay   is

-nakutemo ii desu /   It's okay even if it's not . . .
                   You don't have to . . .

EXAMPLES

Yasukunakutemo | ii   desu. / It's okay even if it's not
              | | cheap.

even if not cheap okay is

Tabenakutemo | ii   desu. / You don't have to eat.
       | | |

if don't eat   okay is

-tewa ikemasen / must not

EXAMPLES

Purezento wa okane | dewa ikemasen. / The gift must
   | | | not (shouldn't)

gift   money   must not be be money.

Tabetewa ikemasen. / You must not eat.

must not eat

-nakutewa ikemasen, -nakereba narimasen / must

EXAMPLES

| Tabenakutewa ikemasen. | / **You must eat.**

       must eat

| Tabenakereba narimasen. | / **You must eat.**

       must eat

> *beki desu* / **should** (obligation), **ought to**

EXAMPLES

Motto | benkyō suru | | beki desu. | / **You should study**
                                      more.
more   study   should

Motto ganbaru | beki desu. | / **You should try harder.**

more try hard should

> *hazu desu* / **is expected** (no moral obligation), **supposition**

EXAMPLES

Mada | nete iru | | hazu desu. | / **He should still be**
                                    sleeping.
still is sleeping should

Kotoshi no natsu Nihon e iku
| | | |
this year 's summer   **go**

| hazu deshita. | / **I was supposed to go to Japan this summer.**
|
was supposed to

> *hō ga ii desu* / **It's better (that) . . .**

EXAMPLES

Motto | benkyō shita | hō ga ii desu. | / **You had better study harder.**
| | |
more   **study**   **had better**

Yasui | hō ga ii desu. | / **The cheap one is better.**
|
cheap   **is better**

> *kamo shirimasen* / **might, probably**

EXAMPLES

Ashita iku | kamo shiremasen. | / **I might go tomorrow.**
| |
tomorrow go   **might**

Mō   tabeta | kamo shiremasen. | / **He might have eaten already.**

already   ate   might

---

hoshii desu / **want, need**

EXAMPLES

Okane ga | hoshii desu. | / **I need money.**

money   need

Kōhī ga | hoshikatta desu. | / **I wanted coffee.**

coffee   wanted

-tai desu / **want**

EXAMPLES

Sushi ga | tabetai desu. | / **I want to eat sushi.**

          want to eat

Sakana wa | tabetaku arimasen. | / **I don't want to eat fish.**

fish   don't want to eat

§8.

Adjectives

§8.1   WHAT ARE ADJECTIVES?

English speakers define *adjectives* as "words which modify or describe nouns."

The Japanese adjective, however, does not fit neatly into the definition of the English adjective. Therefore, speakers of English must be prepared for new ways of looking at adjectives, which in Japanese are quite unlike their English counterparts.

What are the major differences? To put it simply, Japanese adjectives fall into two groups: one group has verb-like characteristics, and the other group has noun-like characteristics. Both groups may function like English adjectives, that is, to modify nouns that follow. With this concept in mind, Japanese adjectives can be understood easily.

One group may be called *verbal adjectives*, the other *adjectival nouns*. We shall look at each group separately. First, the verbal adjectives.

§8.2   VERBAL ADJECTIVES

Adjectives in this group, in their dictionary form, end only in *-ai*, *-ii*, *-oi*, or *-ui*. Thus, they are often referred to as *-i* adjectives.

Here are some common -i adjectives.

-i Adjectives	
chiisai / **small**	takai / **expensive**
yasui / **inexpensive, cheap**	ōkii / **big**
oishii / **delicious**	ii / **good, nice**
yasashii / **easy**	warui / **bad**
atarashii / **new**	muzukashii / **difficult**
omoshiroi / **interesting**	amai / **sweet**
suzushii / **cool**	wakai / **young**
hayai / **fast, early**	itai / **painful**
kuroi / **black**	shiroi / **white**

§8.2-1 Noun Modifiers

The -i adjective in the forms listed above can modify a noun
that follows, just as an English adjective does:

EXAMPLES

chiisai kuruma / **small car**

kuroi kutsu / **black shoes**

omoshiroi hon / **interesting book**

ii hito / **good person**

Atarashii kuruma o | kaimasu. | / **I will buy a new car.**

    new   car   will buy

Oishii kudamono o tabemashita. / **We ate some
delicious fruit.**

       fruit

§8.2-2 Verbal Forms

The forms given in **§8.2** are the dictionary form of the verbal
adjectives. As verbal forms, they have the characteristics of
verbs, as you will see below.

> They have stems.

To form the stem, drop the final -*i*. This is the form used to
make all the other forms of the adjective.

-i Adjective	Stem
akai / **red**	aka-
omoshiroi / **interesting**	omoshiro-
nagai / **long**	naga-
yasui / **cheap**	yasu-

> As is, they form the predicate.

Since the dictionary form is the plain present form of the
verb, you can think of the verbal adjective as already
containing in itself the grammatical form of the copula, or **is**.
And, since a Japanese sentence requires a predicate but
not a subject if the context is clear, each verbal adjective
can constitute a sentence. There can, of course, be other
elements in the sentence.

Note that these are plain forms.

EXAMPLES

Suzushii. / **It's cool.**

Muzukashii. / **It's difficult.**

Atama gai itai. / **My head hurts.**

Kono hon wa, omoshiroi. / **This book is interesting.**

> They conjugate, or change form, for different tenses and moods.

To form the plain past tense, add -katta to the stem.

Plain	
Present	**Past**
suzushii / **is cool**	suzushikatta / **was cool**
oishii / **is delicious**	oishikatta / **was delicious**
chiisai / **is small**	chiisakatta / **was small**
wakai / **is young**	wakakatta / **was young**
osoi / **is slow**	osokatta / **was slow**

To form the negative of the plain present and past, add -ku to the stem. Then, as with regular plain past verbs, add the appropriate form of *nai*.

Plain Negative	
Present	**Past**
suzushiku nai / **isn't cool**	suzushikunakatta / **wasn't cool**
chiisaku nai / **isn't small**	chiisakunakatta / **wasn't small**

For the polite forms, add *desu* to the plain form for the present and the past.

Polite	
Present	**Past**
suzushii desu / **is cool**	suzushikatta desu / **was cool**
chiisai desu / **is small**	chiisakatta desu / **was small**

- To form the polite negative, use the *-ku* form, and add *arimasen* to the present, and *arimasen deshita* to the past.

Polite Negative	
Present	**Past**
suzushiku arimasen / **isn't cool**	suzushiku arimasen deshita/ **wasn't cool**
chiisaku arimasen / **isn't small**	chiisaku arimasen deshita / **wasn't small**

- A variation of the polite negative forms may be formed by adding *desu* to the plain negative forms:

suzushiiku nai desu / **isn't cool**	suzushikunakatta desu / **wasn't cool**
chiisaku nai desu / **isn't small**	chiisakunakatta desu / **wasn't small**

- For other verb moods, the verbal adjective forms can be expanded as follows:

> **Presumptive:** atsui deshō / **will probably be hot**
>
> **Conditional:** atsukereba / **if it were hot**
>
> atsukunakereba / **if it were not hot**
>
> atsukutemo / **even if it's hot**

and so forth (see §7).

The following examples illustrate some uses of the verbal adjective forms presented in this section.

EXAMPLES

Kono kutsu wa, | chiisai desu. | / These shoes are small.

shoes   are small

Ano hon wa, | yasukatta desu. | / That book was cheap.

    was cheap

Hiru gohan wa, | oishikatta desu. | / Lunch was delicious.

lunch   was delicious

Shiken wa | yasashikatta desu. | / The exam was easy.

exam   was easy

Kono kuruma wa, | atarashiku nai desu. | / This car isn't new.

car   isn't new

Sono eiga wa, | omoshiroku arimasen deshita. | / That movie wasn't interesting.

movie   wasn't interesting

Heya wa, | suzushikunakatta desu. | / The room wasn't cool.

room   wasn't cool

§8.2-3 Adverbial Forms

To form adverbs from the *-i* adjectives, just add *-ku* to the stem. Or, to put it another way, change the final *-i* to *-ku*.

Adjective	Adverb
omoshiroi / **interesting**	omoshiroku / **interesting**
hayai / **quick**	hayaku / **quick, quickly**
warui / **bad**	waruku / **bad, badly**
ii / **good**	yoku* / **well**
takai / **expensive**	takaku / **expensive**
kuroi / **black**	kuroku / **black**

*This is an irregular form.

Note how the adverbs are used in sentences. Look at the kinds of verbs typically used with adverbs, especially *naru*, **become**.

EXAMPLES

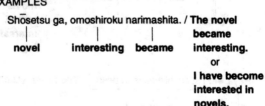

Shōsetsu ga, omoshiroku narimashita. / **The novel became interesting.**
| | | |
novel interesting became

or
I have become interested in novels.

Hayaku ikinasai. / **Go quickly.**

quickly   go

Hayaku arukimashita. / **I walked quickly.**

Tenki ga waruku narimashita. / **The weather became bad.**

weather   bad   became

Tarō san wa, yoku | benkyō shimashita. | / **Taro studied well.**

well   studied

Yachin ga takaku narimashita. / **The rent became expensive.**

rent   expensive became

Doa o kuroku nurimashita. / **I painted the door black.**

door   black painted

Ano hito wa, eigo ga yoku wakarimasu. / **He understands English well.**

English well understands

Yoku nemashita. / **I slept well.**

well   slept

§8.3 ADJECTIVAL NOUNS

Words in this group have noun-like characteristics and can convey adjectival meanings. When they modify nouns, they are followed by the suffix *-na*. Thus, they are often referred to as *-na* adjectives.

Here are some common *-na* adjectives.

-na Adjectives	
shizuka / **quiet**	kirei / **pretty**
genki / **well, healthy**	benri / **convenient**
shinsetsu / **kind**	yūmei / **famous**
jōzu / **good at**	heta / **not good at**
dame / **no good**	suki / **like**
fuben / **inconvenient**	iroiro / **various**
shōjiki / **honest**	teinei / **polite**

You may notice that these words, as translated, do not fit neatly into the English notion of adjectives. The following sections should help clarify their usage.

§8.3-1 Noun Modifiers

With the addition of *-na*, the words in the preceding chart can modify a noun that follows, just as an English adjective does. Notice that for some of the words, the English translation is adjusted slightly to fit this context.

EXAMPLES

    shizukana heya / **quiet room**

kireina hana / **pretty flowers**

genkina hito / **healthy person**

benrina dōgu / **convenient tool**

shinsetsuna sensei / **kind teacher**

yūmeina joyū / **famous actress**

jōzuna kashu / **talented singer**

hetana untenshu / **bad driver**

damena hito / **no good person, bad person**

sukina tabemono / **favorite food**

fubenna jikan / **inconvenient time**

iroirona kuni / **various countries**

shōjikina seijika / **honest politician**

teineina aisatsu / **polite greetings**

This noun modifier construction is similar in form to that of the noun + *no* + noun pattern used to make compound nouns (see §4.8): *eigo no sensei* / **English teacher**, etc. With the adjectival nouns, of course, *-na* is used instead of *no*. Otherwise, the pattern is the same. This is one of the noun-like characteristics of the adjectival nouns.

Now look at some examples of this usage in sentences.

EXAMPLES

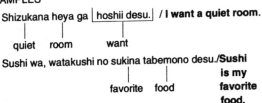

Shizukana heya ga | hoshii desu. | / **I want a quiet room.**

   quiet   room   want

Sushi wa, watakushi no sukina tabemono desu./**Sushi is my favorite food.**

           favorite food

Sore wa fubenna jikan desu. / **That's an inconvenient time.**

inconvenient time

Iroirona kuni ni ikimashita. / **I have visited various countries.**

various countries visited

§8.3-2 Predicate Forms

The adjectival nouns form a predicate as nouns do, by adding the appropriate form of the copula, *desu* / **is, equals** (see §7.6).

Here are the basic forms of *desu*:

desu / **is, equals**		Affirmative	Negative
Present	Plain	da	dewa nai
	Polite	desu	dewa arimasen
Past	Plain	datta	dewa nakatta
	Polite	deshita	dewa arimasen deshita
Presumptive (Probable)	Plain	darō	dewa nai darō
	Polite	deshō	dewa nai deshō

The following examples illustrate how the adjectival nouns plus a form of *desu* constitute the predicate.

EXAMPLES

Kono heya wa, shizuka desu. / **This room is quiet.**
room   quiet

Kōen wa, kirei | dewa arimasen deshita. | / **The park**
wasn't pretty.
park   pretty   wasn't

Chichi wa, genki desu. / **My father is healthy.**
father   healthy

Ano hito wa, supōtsu ga | heta desu. | / **She isn't good**
at sports.
sports   isn't good at

Ano | yakyū no senshu | wa, yūmei desu. / **That baseball**
player is
famous.
baseball player   famous

Sakana wa, | suki dewa arimasen. | / **I don't fish. (Fish**
isn't likable.)
fish   don't like

Jon san wa, Nihon ga suki desu. / **John likes Japan.**
(To John, Japan is
likable.)

Niku wa | dame desu. | / **I don't eat meat. (Meat is no**
good.)
meat   is no good

§8.3-3 Adverbial Forms

To form adverbs from the -na adjectives, use the particle ni after the adjective.

-na Adjective	Adverb
shizuka / **quiet**	shizuka ni / **quiet, quietly**
kirei / **pretty**	kirei ni / **pretty**
genki / **healthy, well**	genki ni / **healthy, well**
shinsetsu / **kind**	shinsetsu ni / **kindly**
teinei / **polite**	teinei ni / **politely**
jōzu / **good at**	jōzu ni / **good at, well**

Look at the adverbial forms in sentences. They are often used with the verbs naru / **become**, and suru / **do**.

EXAMPLES

Kanojo wa, | shizuka ni | arukimasu. / **She walks quietly.**

              quietly   **walks**

Ano hito wa, | teinei ni | hanashimashita. / **He spoke politely.**

              politely   **spoke**

Kanja wa, | genki ni | narimashita. / **The patient became healthy.**

         healthy   **became**

Satō san wa, eigo ga | jōzu ni | narimashita. / **Ms. Sato**
                                                became
                good at   **good at**
                                                English.

Satō san wa, eigo o | jōzu ni | hanashimasu. / **Mr. Sato**
                                                speaks
                  well   **speaks**   **English**
                                                well.

Shizuka ni shinasai. / **Please be quiet.**

  quiet   **do**

§8.4 COMPARISONS

To compare things in Japanese, the adjectives themselves
do not change. Instead, there is a special pattern to learn.
This pattern works for both -*i* adjectives and -*na* adjectives.

To say **A is bigger than B**, the pattern is as follows:

To say **A is cheaper than B**, the pattern is the same:

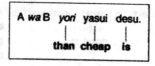

A *wa* B *yori* yasui desu.
       | | |
      than cheap is

EXAMPLES

Budō wa, meron yori yasui desu. / **Grapes are cheaper**
  | | | | | **than melons.**
grapes melons than cheap are

Tōkyō wa, Kyōto yori ōkii desu. / **Tokyo is bigger than**
          | | | **Kyoto.**
        than big is

Kyōto wa, Tōkyō yori chiisai desu. / **Kyoto is smaller**
          | | | **than Tokyo.**
        than small is

To understand clearly which is which in the comparison, the key is the word *yori* / **than**. Focus on this word and the English meaning, and you can quickly sort it out. If you want to say **Oranges are cheaper than apples**, start with **than apples** in English. In Japanese it becomes *ringo yori* / **apples than**, and you can see that **apples** takes the **B** slot in the pattern. The full sentence is as follows:

Orenji wa, ringo yori yasui desu. / **Oranges are**
  | | | | **cheaper than**
oranges apples than cheap are apples.

Another phrase is often used with this pattern, although the meaning remains the same. The words are *no hō*, plus the particle *ga*. The *no* is like the possessive particle used to link the nouns with whatever follows, and *hō* can be translated as **side** or **direction**. The pattern looks like this:

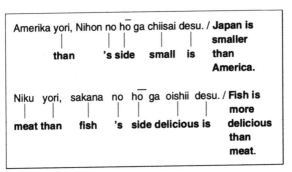

Amerika yori, Nihon no hō ga chiisai desu. / **Japan is smaller than America.**

| than | 's side | small | is |

Niku yori, sakana no hō ga oishii desu. / **Fish is more delicious than meat.**

meat than | fish | 's side | delicious | is

EXAMPLES

Shikago to Tōkyō to, dochira ga suki

or | or which

desu ka. / **Which do you like better, Chicago or Tokyo?**

Tōkyō no hō ga suki desu. / **I like Tokyo better.**

's side | like | is

Jon san to Tomu san to, dare no hō ga wakai

or | or whose | side | younger

desu ka. / **Who is younger, John or Tom?**

is

Jon san no hō ga, wakai desu. / **John is younger.**

        's side   young is

Notice the particle and word order changes in the following two sentences. In the first one, *no hō ga* is used, in the second, *yori* is used alone. Both sentences have the same meaning, but including *no hō ga* makes for stronger contrast in the comparison.

EXAMPLES

Basu yori, chikatetsu no hō ga benri desu. / **The subway is more convenient than the bus.**

Chikatetsu wa, basu yori benri desu. /**The subway is more convenient than the bus.**

 subway   bus than

Another way to answer questions about comparisons is with a simple statement.

EXAMPLES

Ringo to   momo to, dochira ga suki

apples or peaches or which   like

desu ka. / **Which do you like better, apples or peaches?**

Ringo ga suki desu. / **I like apples better.**

Another option is to use the word *motto* which means **more**, for emphasis. It connotes **much (more, better, etc.)**. If you use this with *no hō ga*, the emphasis is even stronger.

EXAMPLES

Ringo ga motto suki desu. / **I like apples much more.**

Ringo no hō ga, motto suki desu. / **I like apples much
more.**

To convey a superlative meaning, use the word *ichiban* /
most, -est, etc.

EXAMPLES

Dono kudamono ga ichiban suki desu ka. / **Which fruit
do you like
best?**

which	fruit	best	like

Banana ga ichiban suki desu. / **I like bananas best.**

Nihon de wa, dono tsuki ga ichiban samui

month	cold

desu ka. / **Which month is the coldest in Japan?**

§8.5 NOMINALIZATION

Adjectives can be *nominalized*, or made into nouns, by a
simple device for each of the two kinds.

For *-i* adjectives, add *-no* to the basic, or dictionary form.

-i Adjective	Noun Form
ōkii / **big**	ōkiino / **big one**
atarashii / **new**	atarashiino / **new one**
hayai / **fast**	hayaino / **fast one**

-*i* Adjective	Noun Form
shiroi / **white**	shiroino / **white one**
amai / **sweet**	amaino / **sweet one**
akai / **red**	akaino / **red one**
kiiroi / **yellow**	kiiroino / **yellow one**

As with English, this form usually occurs in a context, that is, answering a question, or referring to something mutually understood.

EXAMPLES

Ringo o kudasai. / **I want some apples.**

Akaino	to	kiiroino	to,	dochira
red ones	or	yellow ones	or	which

ga ii desu ka. / **Which do you want, red ones or yellow ones?**

Look at two ways of saying the same thing. Note the difference in emphasis.

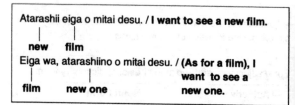

Atarashii eiga o mitai desu. / **I want to see a new film.**

| new | film |

Eiga wa, atarashiino o mitai desu. / **(As for a film), I want to see a new one.**

| film | new one |

Here are some more examples of nominalized adjectives used in sentences:

EXAMPLES

Kēki wa, amaino o kudasai. / **(As for the cake), give me**
   | | **the sweet one.**

cake   sweet one

Hoteru no heya wa, chiisaino ga hoshii desu. / **(As for**
   | | | **a hotel**
hotel   room   small one   **room), I**
                                      want a
                                      small one.

For -na adjectives, add -no to the -na form.

-na Adjective, -na Form	Noun Form
shizukana / **quiet**	shizukanano / **quiet one**
kireina / **pretty**	kireinano / **pretty one**
yūmeina / **famous**	yūmeinano / **famous one**
sukina / **like, favorite**	sukinano / **favorite one**
benrina / **convenient**	benrinano / **convenient one**
teineina / **polite**	teineinano / **polite one, politeness**
hetana / **not good at**	hetanano / **unskillful one**

Here are some sentences with these forms. The uses are
the same as for the -i adjective sentences above.

EXAMPLES

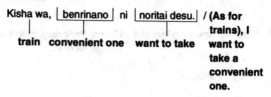

Kisha wa, | benrinano | ni | noritai desu. | / (As for
  train   convenient one   want to take   trains), I
                                        want to
                                        take a
                                        convenient
                                        one.

Kireinano ga | ii desu. | / I want pretty ones.

  pretty ones   want

Teineinano wa taisetsu desu. / **Politeness is important.**

  politeness   important

Adverbs

§9.1 WHAT ARE ADVERBS?

Adverbs are words which modify or describe verbs, adjectives, or other adverbs. They indicate *time*, *place*, *manner*, and *degree*. They answer such questions as **when**, **where**, **how**, and **to what extent**.

As in English, some words in Japanese that are adverbs in one sentence, can be a different part of a speech in another sentence.

EXAMPLES

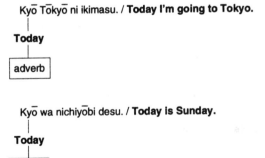

Kyō Tōkyō ni ikimasu. / **Today I'm going to Tokyo.**

Today

adverb

Kyō wa nichiyōbi desu. / **Today is Sunday.**

Today

noun

§9.2 ADVERBS OF PLACE

Some of the demonstrative pronouns (see **§5.5**) function as
adverbs of place.

> koko / **here**
> soko / **there**
> asoko / **over there**

EXAMPLES

Jon san ga, koko ni kimashita. / **John came here.**

     here   **came**

Soko ni / **I want to go there.**

  there   **want to go**

Gakkō wa, asoko ni arimasu. / **The school is over there.**

school **over there**

§9.3 ADVERBS OF TIME

> kinō / **yesterday**
> kyō / **today**
> ashita / **tomorrow**
> mainichi / **every day**
> maiasa / **every morning**
> maiban / **every night**
> ima / **now**
> saikin / **recently**
> yagate / **soon**
> sugu / **immediately**
> mada / **yet, still**

EXAMPLES

Mainichi shinbun o yomimasu. / **I read a newspaper**
every day newspaper   read   **every day.**

Sugu | kite kudasai. | / **Please come immediately.**

immediately please come

Tegami wa, mada desu. / **The mail isn't here yet.**

mail   not yet

Yagate haru ga kimasu. / **Spring will come soon.**

soon spring come

§9.4 ADVERBS OF MANNER AND DEGREE

As in English, adjectives can be made into adverbs of manner and degree:

Adjective	Adverb
hayai / **quick**	hayaku / **quick, quickly**
warui / **bad**	waraku / **bad, badly**
shizuka / **quiet**	shizuka ni / **quiet, quietly**
shinsetsu / **kind**	shinsetsu ni / **kindly**

See **§8.2-3** and **§8.3-3** for more information on the adverbial forms of adjectives.

Some of the demonstrative pronouns are adverbs of manner (see **§5.5**).

> kō / **this way, like this**
> sō / **that way, like that**
> ā / **that way, like that**
> dō / **how**

EXAMPLES

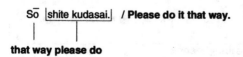

Kō shimashō. / **Let's do it this way.**

this way let's do

Sō shite kudasai. / **Please do it that way.**

that way please do

Ā suru to yoku dekimasu. / **If you do it that way, you can do better.**

that way   if   better   can do

Ōsaka ni wa, dō ikimasu ka. / **How do you get to Osaka?**

how   go

Here are some other adverbs of manner and degree

amari / **not much, not often**	sukoshi / **a little, few**
bakkari / **only**	tabitabi / **often**
chotto / **a little, for a moment**	tabun / **maybe, perhaps, probably**
dandan / **gradually**	taihen / **very (in the sense of extreme degree, positive or negative), greatly**
futsū / **usually**	
hotondo / **almost, all but, hardly**	
ikaga / **how**	taitei / **generally, mainly, perhaps, probably**
itsumo / **always**	takusan / **a lot**
kitto / **certainly, surely**	tamani / **occasionally**
mata / **again**	tokidoki / **sometimes**
minna / **all**	totemo / **very**
mō / **more, already**	yoku / **well, often, much**
motto / **more**	yukkuri / **slowly**
nakanaka / **quite, rather, completely, at all**	zenzen / **at all (with negative verbs)**
	zuibun / **rather, quite**

EXAMPLES

Pan wa, amari | suki dewa arimasen. | / I don't like
                                    bread much.

    much   **don't like**

Chotto | matte kudasai. | / Wait a moment, please.

a moment   **wait**

Meri san wa, itsumo | hataraite imasu. | / Mary is always
                                       working.

    always   **is working**

Mata Amerika e | ikitai desu. | / I want to go to
                                  America again.

again   **want to go**

Mō bangohan o tabemashita. / I ate dinner already.

already dinner   **ate**

Motto arukimashō. / Let's walk some more.

more let's walk

Doitsugo o sukoshi | shitte imasu. | / I know German a
                                  little.

German   **little**   **know**

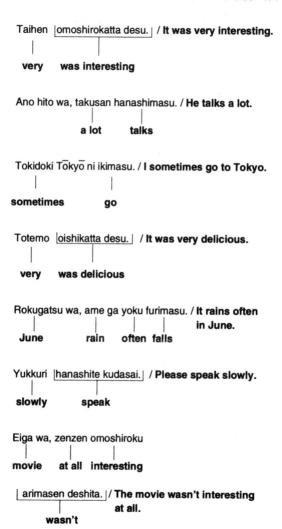

Taihen omoshirokatta desu. / **It was very interesting.**

very   was interesting

Ano hito wa, takusan hanashimasu. / **He talks a lot.**

a lot   talks

Tokidoki Tōkyō ni ikimasu. / **I sometimes go to Tokyo.**

sometimes   go

Totemo oishikatta desu. / **It was very delicious.**

very   was delicious

Rokugatsu wa, ame ga yoku furimasu. / **It rains often in June.**

June   rain   often falls

Yukkuri hanashite kudasai. / **Please speak slowly.**

slowly   speak

Eiga wa, zenzen omoshiroku

movie   at all   interesting

arimasen deshita. / **The movie wasn't interesting at all.**

wasn't

Special Topics

§10.

Numbers

§10.1 CARDINAL NUMBERS

Zero to One Hundred Million

From 1 to 10 only, there are two sets of numbers. The set on the right, of Japanese origin, stops at 10. The set on the left, of Chinese origin, continues indefinitely.

rei	0	
ichi	1	hitotsu
ni	2	futatsu
san	3	mittsu
shi/yon	4	yottsu
go	5	itsutsu
roku	6	muttsu
shichi/nana	7	nanatsu
hachi	8	yattsu
ku/kyū	9	kokonotsu
jū	10	tō

To form numbers from 11 to 19, start with *jū*, 10, and then add the number you need from the column on the left in the preceding chart.

11 jūichi	12 jūni	13 jūsan	14 jūshi/yon	15 jūgo
16 jūroku	17 jūshichi / nana		18 jūhachi	19 jūku

The rest is easy. Twenty is two tens, or *ni jū*, and for 21, just add the 1: *ni jū ichi*.

20 nijū	30 sanjū	40 yonjū	50 gojū
21 nijūichi	31 sanjūichi	41 yonjūichi	51 gojūichi
60 rokujū	70 nanajū	80 hachijū	90 kyūjū
61 rokujūichi	71 nanajūichi	81 hachijūichi	91 kyūjūichi

With 100, *hyaku*, and 1,000, *sen*, the pattern is basically the same, but there are some sound changes, as you will see in the chart below:

100	hyaku		1,000	sen
200	nihyaku		2,000	nisen
300	sanbyaku		3,000	sanzen
400	yonhyaku		4,000	yonsen
500	gohyaku		5,000	gosen
600	roppyaku		6,000	rokusen
700	nanahyaku		7,000	nanasen

800	happyaku	8,000	hassen
900	kyūhyaku	9,000	kyūsen

Japanese uses 10,000 as a counting unit. Each unit of 10,000 is called *man*.

So 10,000 is *ichiman*, 20,000 is *niman*, 100,000 is *jūman*, 200,000 is *nijūman*, 1,000,000 is *hyakuman* (100 units of 10,000). This continues until 100,000,000, *ichi oku*.

§10.2 ORDINAL NUMBERS

The ordinal numbers are formed by adding *banme* to the cardinal numbers.

first	ichibanme	**sixth**	rokubanme
second	nibanme	**seventh**	nanabanme
third	sanbanme	**eighth**	hachibanme
fourth	yonbanme	**ninth**	kyūbanme
fifth	gobanme	**tenth**	jūbanme

To continue, follow the pattern for the cardinal numbers, adding *banme*. **Eleventh** is *jūichibanme*, **twelfth** is *jūnibanme*, and so forth.

§11.

Telling Time

To express time in Japanese, we start with a list of the
hours, then a list of the **minutes**, and then we put them
together.

Here are the **hours**:

1 o'clock	ichiji	7 o'clock	shichiji
2 o'clock	niji	8 o'clock	hachiji
3 o'clock	sanji	9 o'clock	kuji
4 o'clock	yoji	10 o'clock	jūji
5 o'clock	goji	11 o'clock	jūichiji
6 o'clock	rokuji	12 o'clock	jūniji

Now the **minutes**:

1 minute	ippun	10 minutes	juppun
2 minutes	nifun	11 minutes	jūippun
3 minutes	sanpun	12 minutes	jūnifun
4 minutes	yonpun	13 minutes	jūsanpun
5 minutes	gofun	14 minutes	jūyonpun
6 minutes	roppun	15 minutes	jūgofun
7 minutes	nanafun	16 minutes	jūroppun
8 minutes	happun	17 minutes	jūnanafun
9 minutes	kyūfun	18 minutes	jūhappun

19 minutes	jūkyūfun	24 minutes	nijūyonpun
20 minutes	nijuppun	25 minutes	nijūgofun
21 minutes	nijūippun	30 minutes	sanjuppun
22 minutes	nijūnifun	40 minutes	yonjuppun
23 minutes	nijūsanpun	50 minutes	gojuppun

Now we can put them together. Say the hour first, then the minutes, then add *desu*:

EXAMPLES

Nanji desu ka. / **What time is it?**

Jūji jūgofun desu. / **It's 10:15.**

- Using *sugi*, which means **past** or **after**, is optional.

Jūji jūgofun sugi desu. / **It's 10:15.**

|
after

- At 15 minutes before the hour, start using *mae*, which means **to** or **before**.

Jūji jūgofun mae desu. / **It's a quarter to ten.**

|
before

- *Han* means **half**, as in **half past** the hour.

Goji desu.	It's 5 o'clock.
Goji gofun desu.	It's 5:05.
Goji juppun desu.	It's 5:10.
Goji jūgofun desu.	It's 5:15.
Goji nijuppun desu.	It's 5:20.
Goji nijūgofun desu.	It's 5:25.
Goji han desu.	It's 5:30.
Goji sanjūgofun desu.	It's 5:35.
Goji yonjuppun desu.	It's 5:40.
Goji yonjūgofun desu.	It's 5:45.
Rokuji jūgofun mae desu.	It's a quarter to six.
Rokuji juppun mae desu.	It's 5:50/ten to six.
Rokuji gofun mae desu.	It's 5:55/five to six.

Gozen is A.M. *Gogo* is P.M. Say them *before* you say the hour.

EXAMPLES

Gozen kuji desu. / It's 9 A.M.

A.M.

Gogo jūji desu. / It's 10 P.M.

P.M.

For time schedules, as in railway and airline timetables, numbers 1 to 59 are used for minutes, *not* **a quarter to** or **ten to** the hour.

Transportation timetables are based on the 24-hour clock. Airline and train schedules are expressed in terms of a point within a 24-hour sequence.

EXAMPLES

Watakushi no kisha wa, jūsanji yonjūhappun ni demasu. / **My train departs at 13:48.**

Watakushi no hikōki wa, jūji gojūsanpun ni tsukimasu. / **My plane arrives at 10:53.**

Classifiers

To count things in Japanese, you use special classifiers, or counters. Here are some of the most common ones:

Counting Different Kinds of Things

People				
1 hitori	2 futari	3 sannin	4 yonin	5 gonin
6 rokunin	7 nananin	8 hachinin	9 kunin	10 jūnin

Long, thin objects (pencils, bottles, trees, etc.)				
1 ippon	2 nihon	3 sanbon	4 yonhon	5 gohon
6 roppon	7 nanahon	8 happon	9 kyūhon	10 juppon

Bound objects (books, magazines, notebooks, etc.)				
1 issatsu	2 nisatsu	3 sansatsu	4 yonsatsu	5 gosatsu
6 rokusatsu	7 nanasatsu	8 hassatsu	9 kyūsatsu	10 jussatsu

Thin, flat objects (paper, bills, cloth, tickets, dishes, etc.)				
1 ichimai	2 nimai	3 sanmai	4 yomai	5 gomai
6 rokumai	7 nanamai	8 hachimai	9 kyūmai	10 jūmai

Liquid or dry measures (glasses or cups of water, coffee, tea, etc.)

1 ippai	2 nihai	3 sanbai	4 yonhai	5 gohai
6 roppai	7 nanahai	8 happai	9 kyūhai	10 juppai

Houses, buildings, etc.

1 ikken	2 niken	3 sangen	4 yonken	5 goken
6 rokken	7 nanaken	8 hakken	9 kyūken	10 jukken

Small objects not in categories listed above (apples, candy, etc.)

1 ikko / hitotsu	2 niko / futatsu	3 sanko / mittsu
4 yonko / yottsu	5 goko / itsutsu	6 rokko / muttsu
7 nanako / nanatsu	8 hakko / yattsu	9 kyūko / kokonotsu
10 jukko / tō		

Floors of buildings

1 ikkai	2 nikai	3 sangai	4 yonkai	5 gokai
6 rokkai	7 nanakai	8 hakkai	9 kyūkai	10 jukkai

Animals, fish, insects

1 ippiki	2 nihiki	3 sanbiki	4 yonhiki	5 gohiki
6 roppiki	7 nanahiki	8 happiki	9 kyūhiki	10 juppiki

§13.

Days, Months, Seasons, the Weather

§13.1 DAYS OF THE WEEK

getsuyōbi / **Monday**   mokuyōbi / **Thursday**

kayōbi / **Tuesday**   kinyōbi / **Friday**

suiyōbi / **Wednesday**   doyōbi / **Saturday**

nichiyōbi / **Sunday**

asa / **morning** gogo / **afternoon**
yugata / **evening** yoru / **night**

Related Expressions

Kyō wa, nani yōbi desu ka. / **What day is today?**

Kyō wa, _____ desu. / **It's _____.**

ichinichi / **day**	ashita / **tomorrow**
kyō / **today**	asatte / **the day after**
kinō / **yesterday**	**tomorrow**
ototoi / **the day before**	shū / **week**
yesterday	konshū / **this week**

raishū / **next week**	yūgata / **in the early evening**
isshūkan / **for one week**	yoru / **in the evening**
nishūkan / **for two weeks**	asa made ni / **by morning**
isshūkan de / **in one week**	kayōbi made ni / **by Tuesday**
nishūkan de / **in two weeks**	heijitsu / **weekday**
futsuka kan / **for two days**	shūmatsu / **weekend**
ichi nichi de / **in one day**	mainichi / **every day**
futsuka de / **in two days**	kyō kara isshūkan go / **a week from today**
mikka mae / **three days ago**	
kesa / **this morning**	kyō kara / **from today on**
kyō no gogo / **this afternoon**	yasumi / **day off**
konban / **tonight**	kyūjitsu / **holiday**
ashita no ban / **tomorrow night**	shigoto bi / **work day**
	ichinichi ni tsuki / **per day**
gozen chū / **in the morning**	kyō jū ni / **during the day**
gogo / **in the afternoon**	konshū jū ni / **during the week**

§13.2 MONTHS OF THE YEAR

ichigatsu / **January**	shichigatsu / **July**
nigatsu / **February**	hachigatsu / **August**
sangatsu / **March**	kugatsu / **September**
shigatsu / **April**	jūgatsu / **October**
gogatsu / **May**	jūichigatsu / **November**
rokugatsu / **June**	jūnigatsu / **December**

Days, Months, Seasons, the Weather **183**

§13.3 DAYS OF THE MONTH

tsuitachi / **1st**	jūrokunichi / **16th**
futsuka / **2nd**	jūshichinichi / **17th**
mikka / **3rd**	jūhachinichi / **18th**
yokka / **4th**	jūkunichi / **19th**
itsuka / **5th**	hatsuka / **20th**
muika / **6th**	nijūichinichi / **21st**
nanoka / **7th**	nijūninichi / **22nd**
yōka / **8th**	nijūsannichi / **23rd**
kokonoka / **9th**	nijūyokka / **24th**
tōka / **10th**	nijūgonichi / **25th**
jūichinichi / **11th**	nijūrokunichi / **26th**
jūninichi / **12th**	nijūshichinichi / **27th**
jūsannichi / **13th**	nijūhachinichi / **28th**
jūyokka / **14th**	nijūkunichi / **29th**
jūgonichi / **15th**	sanjūnichi / **30th**
	sanjūichinichi / **31st**

§13.4 COUNTING DAYS

ichinichi / **one day**	itsuka / **five days**
futsuka / **two days**	muika / **six days**
mikka / **three days**	nanoka / **seven days**
yokka / **four days**	yōka / **eight days**

kokonoka / **nine days**	jūichinichi / **eleven days**
tōka / **ten days**	jūninichi / **twelve days**

Related Expressions

Nikagetsu mae / **2 months ago**

sengetsu / **last month**

kongetsu / **this month**

raigetsu / **next month**

_____ gatsu chū ni / **during the month of** _____

_____ gatsu irai / **since the month of** _____

_____ gatsu ni / **for the month of** _____

mai tsuki / **every month**

ikkagetsu ni tsuki / **per month**

ikkagetsu / **one month**

sūkagetsu / **a few months**

Kyō wa, nan nichi desu ka. / **What's today's date?**

Kyō wa, _____ desu. / **Today is** _____.

gogatsu, tsuitachi, getsuyōbi / **Monday, May 1**

rokugatsu futsuka, kayōbi / **Tuesday, June 2**

Note: For these expressions, use the days of the month listed in §13.3.

§13.5 SEASONS

fuyu / **winter**	natsu / **summer**
haru / **spring**	aki / **fall**

Related Expressions

Fuyu desu. / **It's winter.**

Haru desu. / **It's spring.**

Natsu desu. / **It's summer.**

Aki desu. / **It's fall.**

§13.6 THE WEATHER

Tenki wa dō desu ka. / **How's the weather?**
Samui desu. / **It's cold.**
Totemo samui desu. / **It's very cold.**
Yuki ga futte imasu. / **It's snowing.**
Atatakai desu. / **It's warm.**
Hi ga tette imasu. / **It's sunny.**
Atsui desu. / **It's hot.**
Shikke ga takai desu. / **It's humid.**
Mushiatsui desu. / **It's hot and humid.**
Ii tenki desu. / **It's a beautiful day.**
Ame ga futte imasu. / **It's raining.**
Arashi desu. / **It's stormy.**
Kaminari ga natte, inazuma ga hikatte imasu. / **It's thundering and lightning.**
Suzushii desu. / **It's cool.**
Kiri desu. / **It's foggy.**
Ame ga, hageshiku futte imasu. / **It's raining heavily.**

Family Relationships

Choose a term from the appropriate column in the chart below when talking about family members. In Japanese, the terms for family relationships differ according to whether you are talking about your own family to someone else, or about the other person's family. You refer to your own family with a set of neutral forms, to another person's family with a set of honorific terms.

Family Member	Talking about Your Family	Talking about Another's Family
grandfather	sofu	ojiisan
grandmother	sobo	obāsan
father	chichi	otōsan
mother	haha	okāsan
husband	otto/shujin	goshujin
wife	tsuma	okusan
uncle	oji	ojisan
aunt	oba	obasan
son	musuko	musukosan
daughter	musume	ojōsan
cousin	itoko	itoko
elder brother	ani	oniisan
younger brother	otōto	otōtosan

Family Member	Talking about Your Family	Talking about Another's Family
elder sister	ane	onēsan
younger sister	imōto	imōtosan

§15.

Useful Words and Phrases

You will find this section useful in communicating with the Japanese. Just find the category you want, and choose the expression you need!

§15.1 GREETINGS

To begin, you should know that Japanese does not have a word that is the equivalent of the English word **Hello**. Instead, use the words for **Good morning**, **Good afternoon**, etc.

Ohayō gozaimasu. / **Good morning.**
Konnichiwa. / **Good afternoon.**
Konbanwa. / **Good evening.**
Oyasuminasai. / **Good night.** (This is used at the end of the evening, or at bedtime.)
Sayōnara. / **Goodbye.**

Japanese has no equivalent for the English expression **How are you?** that is used as a daily greeting. The following expression is used only when you have not seen someone for a while.

Ogenki desu ka. / **How are you?**
Hai, okagesama de. / **Fine, thank you.**

§15.2 COMMON EXPRESSIONS

You will find these expressions handy in daily life.

Hai. / **Yes.**

Iie. / **No.**

san / **Mr., Mrs., Miss, Ms.**

Dōmo arigatō. / **Thank you.**

Iie, dō itashimashite. /
You're welcome.

Sumimasen. / **I'm sorry.**

Gomennasai. / **Excuse me.**

Onegai shimasu. / **Please.**

Dōzo. / **Please.**

Moshi moshi. / **Hello.** (This is
used for telephone calls, or
for getting someone's
attention.)

Sumimasen ga. / **Pardon
me, but _____.**

Daijōbu desu. / **It's all right.**

Yorokonde. / **With pleasure.**

Ii desu yo. / **I don't mind.**

Ā, sō desu ka. / **Oh, I see.**

Ikimashō ka. / **Shall we go?**

Sā. / **Let's (go/eat/etc.)**

Iie, kekkō desu. / **No, thank
you.**

Sō da to omoimasu. / **I think
so.**

Sō omoimasen. / **I don't
think so.**

Omoshiroi desu. / **It's
interesting.**

Owarimashita. / **It's over /
I'm finished.**

Hai, sō desu. / **Yes, it is.**

Iie, chigaimasu. / **No, it isn't.**

Chotto, matte kudasai. / **Just
a moment, please.**

Sugu, onegai shimasu. /
Right away. (request)

Soredewa nochi hodo. / **See
you later.**

Soredewa mata ashita. / **See you tomorrow.**

Wakarimasu ka. / **Do you understand?**

Hai, wakarimasu. / **Yes, I understand.**

Iie, wakarimasen. / **No, I don't understand.**

Eigo ga wakarimasu ka. / **Do you understand English?**

Nihongo ga, sukoshi hanasemasu. / **I speak a little Japanese.**

Nihongo wa, wakarimasen. / **I don't understand Japanese.**

Mō ichido onegai shimasu. / **Could you repeat it, please?**

Mō sukoshi, yukkuri hanshite kudasai. / **Please speak slowly.**

Eigo o hanashimasu ka. / **Do you speak English?**

Kore wa, Nihongo de nan to iimasu ka. / **What's this called in Japanese?**

Kore wa, nan to iimasu ka. / **What do you call this?**

Sumimasen ga, tasukete itadakemasen ka. / **Excuse me, could you help me, please?**

§15.3 SOME QUESTIONS AND QUESTION WORDS

Dō ka, shimashita ka. / **What's the matter?**

Kore wa, nan desu ka. / **What's this?**

Itsu. / **When?**

Doko. / **Where?**

Naze. / Dōshite. / **Why?**

Dare. / Donata. / **Who?**

Dore. / Dochira. / **Which?**

Nani. / **What?**

Dono kurai. / **How much?**

Ikura. / **How much (money)?**

§15.4 YOUR PERSONAL CONDITION

> Nodo ga, kawaite imasu. / **I'm thirsty.**
> Onaka ga, suite imasu. / **I'm hungry.**
> Onaka ga, ippai desu. / **I'm full.**
> Tsukarete imasu. / **I'm tired.**
> Nemui desu. / **I'm sleepy.**
> Byōki desu. / **I'm sick.**
> Genki desu. / **I'm fine.**
> Daijōbu desu. / **I'm all right.**

§15.5 INTRODUCTIONS

Proper introductions are important in Japan. When possible, it's preferable to have a Japanese friend introduce you to another Japanese. If not, you will find the expressions you need below.

Ano kata wa, donata desu ka. / **Who is that?**

Ano kata wa, donata ka gozonji desu ka. / **Do you know who that is?**

Ano kata ni, ome ni kakaritai no desu ga. / **I would like to meet him / her.**

Ano kata ni, shōkai shite itadakemasen ka. / **Would you introduce me to him / her?**

Totsuzen shitsurei desu ga, jiko shōkai shitemo yoroshii desu ka. / **Pardon me, may I introduce myself?**

Watakushi no namae wa _____desu. / **My name is**

_____

Anata no onomae wa. / **What's your name?**

Hajimemashite. Dōzo yoroshiku. / **How do you do?**

Hajimemashite. Kochira koso yoroshiku. / **How do you do?**
  (reply)

Ome ni kakarete, kōei desu. / **I'm honored to meet you.**

Yoroshiku onegai shimasu. / **I'm glad to meet you.**

meishi / **business card**

Meishi o dōzo. / **Here's my card.**

Arigatō gozaimasu. / **Thank you very much.**

Watakushi no mo dōzo. / **Here's mine.**

Meishi o chōdai dekimasu ka. / **May I have your card?**

§16.

Borrowed Words

Countless words borrowed from English are in everyday use in Japan. But even for an English speaker, there are pitfalls. Why? With borrowed words in Japan, you can never assume that they have made the trip across the Pacific intact.

> Trust These!

These words *are* what they seem. If you can understand the pronunciation, you have the meaning.

orenji / **orange**	bīru / **beer**
kōhī / **coffee**	pinku / **pink**
poketto / **pocket**	gasorin / **gasoline**
takushī / **taxi**	basu / **bus**
rajio / **radio**	tomato / **tomato**
banana / **banana**	batā / **butter**
kukkī / **cookie**	sūpu / **soup**
reinkōto / **raincoat**	beddo / **bed**

Careful!

Some element in each of these words connects it to the original meaning.

wāpuro / **word processor**	depāto / **department store**
pasokon / **personal computer**	hankachi / **handkerchief**
waishatsu / **dress shirt**	irasuto / **illustration**
sūpā / **supermarket**	amefuto / **American football**
basuke / **basketball**	
puro / **professional**	

Made in Japan!

With words like these, all bets are off. Don't even think of them as coming from English. How different *are* they? If you are invited for *mōningu baikingu*, don't put on your biking clothes. You are going for a smorgasbord breakfast, *not* morning biking!

baikingu / **smorgasbord (Viking)**
mōningu baikingu / **smorgasbord breakfast**
keki baikingu / **dessert smorgasbord**
manshon / **condominium**
manshon refomu / **condominium renovations**
spaman / **condominium at a hot springs resort**
  (spa + manshon)
wanpīsu / **dress (one piece)**

Verb Charts

In the following charts you will find conjugated forms of a sample of Japanese verbs.

hanasu / **to speak**

Stem: hanas-

		Affirmative	Transitive Negative
Present:	Plain	hanasu	hanasanai
	Polite	hanashimasu	hanashimasen
Past:	Plain	hanashita	hanasanakatta
	Polite	hanashimashita	hanashimasen deshita
Gerund (-te form:)		hanashite	hanasanaide hanasanakute
Presumptive:	Plain	hanasu darō	hanasanai darō
	Polite	hanasu deshō	hanasanai deshō
	Plain	hanasō	hanasumai
	Polite	hanashimashō	
Imperative:	Plain	hanase	hanasuna
	Polite	hanashite kudasai	hanasanaide kudasai
Conditional:		hanaseba	hanasanakereba
		hanashitara	hanasanakattara

Plain Affirmative

Potential:	hanaseru	Honorific:	ohanashi ni naru
Passive:	hanasareru		ohanashi nasaru
Causative:	hanasaseru	Humble:	ohanashi suru
			ohanashi itasu
Causative Passive:	hanasaserareru		

iku / **to go**

Stem: ik-			Intransitive
		Affirmative	Negative
Present:	Plain	iku	ikanai
	Polite	ikimasu	ikimasen
Past:	Plain	itta	ikanakatta
	Polite	ikimashita	ikimasen deshita
Gerund (-*te* form):		itte	ikanaide ikanakute
Presumptive:	Plain	iku darō	ikanai darō
	Polite	iku deshō	ikanai deshō
	Plain	ikō	ikumai
	Polite	ikimashō	
Imperative:	Plain	ike	ikuna
	Polite	itte kudasai	ikanaide kudasai
Conditional:		ikeba	ikanakereba
		ittara	ikanakattara

Plain Affirmative			
Potential:	ikeru	Honorific:	irassharu
Passive:	ikareru		
Causative:	ikaseru	Humble:	mairu
Causative Passive:	ikaserareru		

kaeru / **to return**

Stem: kaer-			Intransitive
		Affirmative	Negative
Present:	Plain	kaeru	kaeranai
	Polite	kaerimasu	kaerimasen
Past:	Plain	kaetta	kaeranakatta
	Polite	kaerimashita	kaerimasen deshita
Gerund (-*te* form):		kaette	kaeranaide kaeranakute
Presumptive:	Plain	kaeru darō	kaeranai darō
	Polite	kaeru deshō	kaeranai deshō
	Plain	kaerō	kaerumai
	Polite	kaerimashō	
Imperative:	Plain	kaere	kaeruna
	Polite	kaette kudasai	kaeranaide kudasai
Conditional:		kaereba kaettara	kaeranakereba kaeranakattara

Plain Affirmative

Potential:	kaereru	Honorific:	okaeri ni naru
Passive:	kaerareru		okaeri nasaru
Causative:	kaeraseru	Humble:	_____
Causative Passive:	kaeraserareru		

kau / **to buy**

Stem: ka-			Transitive
		Affirmative	Negative
Present:	Plain	kau	kawanai
	Polite	kaimasu	kaimasen
Past:	Plain	katta	kawanakatta
	Polite	kaimashita	kaimasen deshita
Gerund (-te form):		katte	kawanaide kawanakute
Presumptive:	Plain	kau darō	kawanai darō
	Polite	kau deshō	kawanai deshō
	Plain	kaō	kaumai
	Polite	kaimashō	
Imperative:	Plain	kae	kauna
	Polite	katte kudasai	kawanaide kudasai
Conditional:		kaeba	kawanakereba
		kattara	kawanakattara

Plain Affirmative

Potential:	kaeru	Honorific:	okai ni naru
Passive:	kawareru		okai nasaru
Causative:	kawaseru	Humble:	okai suru
Causative Passive:	kawaserareru		okai itasu

kiku / to listen, to ask, to hear

Stem: kik-			Transitive
		Affirmative	Negative
Present:	Plain	kiku	kikanai
	Polite	kikimasu	kikimasen
Past:	Plain	kiita	kikanakatta
	Polite	kikimashita	kikimasen deshita
Gerund (-te form):		kiite	kikanaide kikanakute
Presumptive:	Plain	kiku darō	kikanai darō
	Polite	kiku deshō	kikanai deshō
	Plain	kikō	kikumai
	Polite	kikimashō	
Imperative:	Plain	kike	kikuna
	Polite	kiite kudasai	kikanaide kudasai
Conditional:		kikeba	kikanakereba
		kiitara	kikanakattara

Plain Affirmative

Potential:	kikeru	Honorific:	okiki ni naru
Passive:	kikareru		okiki nasaru
Causative:	kikaseru	Humble:	ukagau (to ask)
Causative Passive:	kikaserareru		okiki suru (to ask)

kuru / to come

Stem: ku-			Intransitive
		Affirmative	Negative
Present:	Plain	kuru	konai
	Polite	kimasu	kimasen
Past:	Plain	kita	konakatta
	Polite	kimashita	kimasen deshita
Gerund (-te form):		kite	konaide konakute
Presumptive:	Plain	kuru darō	konai darō
	Polite	kuru deshō	konai deshō
	Plain	koyō	kurumai
	Polite	kimashō	
Imperative:	Plain	koi	kuruna
	Polite	kite kudasai	konaide kudasai
Conditional:		kureba	konakereba
		kitara	konakattara

Plain Affirmative

Potential:	korareru	Honorific:	irassharu
Passive:	korareru		oide ni naru
Causative:	kosaseru	Humble:	mairu
Causative Passive:	kosaserareru		

miru / **to look at, to see**

Stem: mi-			Transitive
		Affirmative	Negative
Present:	Plain	miru	minai
	Polite	mimasu	mimasen
Past:	Plain	mita	minakatta
	Polite	mimashita	mimasen deshita
Gerund (-te form):		mite	minaide
			minakute
Presumptive:	Plain	miru darō	minai darō
	Polite	miru deshō	minai deshō
	Plain	miyō	mimai
	Polite	mimashō	
Imperative:	Plain	miro	miruna
	Polite	mite kudasai	minaide kudasai
Conditional:		mireba	minakereba
		mitara	minakattara

Plain Affirmative

Potential:	mirareru	Honorific:	goran ni naru
Passive:	mirareru		goran nasaru
Causative:	misaseru	Humble:	haiken suru
Causative Passive:	misaserareru		haiken itasu

nomu / to drink

Stem: nom-			Transitive
		Affirmative	Negative
Present:	Plain	nomu	nomanai
	Polite	nomimasu	nomimasen
Past:	Plain	nonda	nomanakatta
	Polite	nomimashita	nomimasen deshita
Gerund (-te form):		nonde	nomanaide
			nomanakute
Presumptive:	Plain	nomu darō	nomanai darō
	Polite	nomu deshō	nomanai deshō
	Plain	nomō	nomumai
	Polite	nomimashō	
Imperative:	Plain	nome	nomuna
	Polite	nonde kudasai	nomanaide kudasai
Conditional:		nomeba	nomanakereba
		nondara	nomanakattara

Plain Affirmative

Potential:	nomeru	Honorific:	onomi ni naru
Passive:	nomareru		onomi nasaru
Causative:	nomaseru	Humble:	itadaku
Causative Passive:	nomaserareru		

suru / **to do, to make**

Stem: su-			Transitive
		Affirmative	Negative
Present:	Plain	suru	shinai
	Polite	shimasu	shimasen
Past:	Plain	shita	shinakatta
	Polite	shimashita	shimasen deshita
Gerund (-*te* form):		shite	shinaide shinakute
Presumptive:	Plain	suru darō	shinai darō
	Polite	suru deshō	shinai deshō
	Plain	shiyō	surumai
	Polite	shimashō	
Imperative:	Plain	shiro	suruna
	Polite	shite kudasai	shinaide kudasai
Conditional:		sureba	shinakereba
		shitara	shinakattara

Plain Affirmative

Potential:	dekiru	Honorific:	nasaru
Passive:	sareru		
Causative:	saseru	Humble:	itasu
Causative Passive:	saserareru		

taberu / to eat

Stem: tabe-			Transitive
		Affirmative	Negative
Present:	Plain	taberu	tabenai
	Polite	tabemasu	tabemasen
Past:	Plain	tabeta	tabenakatta
	Polite	tabemashita	tabemasen deshita
Gerund (-te form):		tabete	tabenaide tabenakute
Presumptive:	Plain	taberu darō	tabenai darō
	Polite	taberu deshō	tabenai deshō
	Plain	tabeyō	tabemai
	Polite	tabemashō	
Imperative:	Plain	tabero	taberuna
	Polite	tabete kudasai	tabenaide kudasai
Conditional:		tabereba tabetara	tabenakereba tabenakattara

Plain Affirmative

Potential	taberareru	Honorific:	meshiagaru
Passive:	taberareru		otabe ni naru
Causative:	tabesaseru		otabe nasaru
Causative Passive:	tabesaserareru	Humble:	itadaku

wakaru / **to understand**

Stem: wakar-			Intransitive
		Affirmative	Negative
Present:	Plain	wakaru	wakaranai
	Polite	wakarimasu	wakarimasen
Past:	Plain	wakatta	wakaranakatta
	Polite	wakarimashita	wakarimasen deshita
Gerund (-*te* form):		wakatte	wakaranaide wakaranakute
Presumptive:	Plain	wakaru darō	wakaranai darō
	Polite	wakaru deshō	wakaranai deshō
	Plain	wakarō	wakarumai
	Polite	wakarimashō	
Imperative:	Plain	wakare	
	Polite	wakatte kudasai	
Conditional:		wakareba	wakaranakereba
		wakattara	wakaranakattara

Plain Affirmative

Potential:	_____	Honorific:	owakari ni naru
Passive:	_____		owakari nasaru
Causative:	wakaraseru	Humble:	_____
Causative Passive:	wakaraserareru		

Index

References in this index to the Basics, the Parts of Speech, and Special Topics are indicated by the symbol § followed by the decimal number.

2500 x 2.25 x 2 =